I Explore

A Science Textbook

4

Mrinalini Pradhan

CAMBRIDGE
UNIVERSITY PRESS

CAMBRIDGE UNIVERSITY PRESS
Cambridge, New York, Melbourne, Madrid, Cape Town, Singapore,
São Paulo, Delhi, Dubai, Tokyo

Cambridge University Press
4381/4 Ansari Road, Daryaganj, Delhi 110002, India

www.cambridge.org
Information on this title: www.cambridge.org/9780521185790 Paperback
www.cambridge.org/9780521185745 Paperback with CD-ROM

First published 2011
Reprinted in 2011 (twice), 2012

Printed in India at Manipal Technologies Limited, Manipal

A catalogue for this publication is available from the British Library

ISBN 978-0-521-18579-0 Paperback
ISBN 978-0-521-18574-5 Paperback with CD-ROM

Additional resources for this publication at www.cambridgeindia.org

Contents

Overview

Lesson	Topic	Syllabus	Objectives	Activities
Unit 1: Food				
1.	Food	Nutrients. A balanced diet. Alertness concerning food.	Recalls the different types of food. Recognizes the different nutrients present in food and their functions. Understands the importance of a balanced diet. Practises proper food habits. Appreciates the need of cleaning, cooking and preserving food.	Draw four different types of food you eat every day in the boxes. Select food from the food pyramid and write your menu for a Sunday. Visit a market with your parents. Tell them what food items to choose and why. Note down for a week what you eat in your meals. Write the nutrients present in it and whether your diet was a balanced diet.
2.	Teeth and Digestion	Our teeth. Types of teeth. Structure of a tooth. Care of teeth. Digestion of food. Process of digestion. Good eating habits.	Understands the importance of teeth. Distinguishes the different types of teeth. Learns the structure of a tooth. Practises proper care of teeth. Learns the names of digestive organs. Understands how food is broken into simpler form. Practises good eating habits.	Write a slogan and a caption for the picture. Find out and note down the number of milk and permanent teeth each child in your class has. Fill two glasses with water. Add a teaspoon of wheat flour to one glass and one teaspoon of sugar to another glass. Stir the water in both the glasses and check their solubility. Draw a series of pictures showing how a healthy tooth decays. Make banners showing how to take care of the teeth. Write a jingle next to it. Obseve the different types of tooth problems of the patients. Record the treatment prescribed by the dentist
Unit 2: Materials				
3.	Safety	Safety at home. Safety at school. Safety on the playground. Safety on road. Rail safety tips. First aid.	Learns how accidents are caused. Understands how accidents can be avoided. Gains knowledge of the measures to be taken in case the cooking gas starts leaking. Follows rail safety tips.	Name and draw the safety gear common in all the pictures. Stand at the window for fifteen minutes and note down how many people ride the two wheeler without wearing the helmet. Read the newspaper for a week and note down how many accidents have occurred due to carelessness and discuss how they could have been avoided. Prepare a project on road traffic symbols used to prevent road
4.	Clothes and Fibres	Sources of fibres. Natural fibres. Animal fibres. Synthetic fibres. Clothes and climates.	Learns what is fibre and how cloth is made. Differentiates between natural and synthetic fibres. Learns how silk and woollen fibre is obtained. Understands that clothes worn by people depend on the climate.	Tick mark the things on the picture made of cloth. Make two groups. First group acts as manufacturers of natural fibres and puts up PowerPoint presentation to convince that their fibres are superior. The second group does the same for synthetic fibres. Find out and write differences between clothes worn by a farmer and a factory worker. Write and paste photographs of the clothes you wear at home, while playing, in school and attending wedding.
5.	Houses All Around	Types of houses depend on: climate, building material, budget. People who build a house.	Recalls the names of people who build a house with the help of the tools they use. Learns that the houses built depend on the climate, building material and the budget. Understands that many people put in efforts to build a proper house. Realizes that care of the house should be taken once it is built.	Name the persons who use the given tools to build a house. Design and draw the house you would like to live in. Make a house using different types of materials. Find out the living conditions of a person who does not have a proper house to live in.
6.	Solids, Liquids and Gases	Matter. States of matter. States of matter are interchangeable. Solubility.	Learns what is matter and the arrangement of molecules in different states of matter. Understands that states of matter are interchangeable. Gains knowledge about solubility and learns what is solute, solvent and solution. Conducts simple experiments.	Write what the given things are made of. Write H for soilds which are hard and S for solids which are soft. Experiment to show that liquids have a definite volume. Experiment to show that gases take up all the space available. Experiments showing solubility of sugar and sand. Test the solubility of the given substances. Write an experiment showing the preparation of lemon juice.
Unit 3: The World of the Living				
7.	Plants—Making Food	Parts of a leaf. How is food made in the leaves. Energy flow in living things. Animals and plants depend on each other.	Recognizes the internal structure of a leaf. Understands the process of photosynthesis. Understands the interdependence between plants and animals. Conducts simple experiments.	Paste a leaf and write its shape, colour, texture and the kind of edge. Experiment to show that stored food in potato is starch. Find out and write what green plants give us. Draw a diagram of photosynthesis and make banners on "Grow More Trees" and "Save Trees".

Overview

esson	Topic	Syllabus	Objectives	Activities
8.	Adaptations in Plants	Terrestrial plants in hilly areas, plains, hot and damp areas, deserts, marshy areas; Aquatic plants—floating, fixed and underwater plants. Unusual plants.	Learns what is adaptations in plants. Identifies different plants on the basis of their habitat. Gains knowledge about some unusual plants.	Choose the correct option for each of the given options. Collect information on some unusual plants and write how they adapt to their surroundings. Prepare a project on plants and animals found in a rainforest.
9.	Adaptations in Animals	Adaptations to habitat—terrestrial, aquatic, amphibian, aerial and arboreal. Adaptations for food—herbivores, carnivores, omnivores, parasites. Adaptations for protection.	Understands the importance of adaptations in animals. Classifies animals on the basis of their habitat and feeding habits. Learns how some animals adapt to protect themselves from enemies.	Find the animals hiding in the pictures. Identify the animals with the given adaptive features. Draw or paste pictures and write information about behavioural adaptations of two animals. Make a chart of animals that adapt themselves by blending in the surroundings. Make a chart on adaptive features of a camel.

Unit 4: Moving Things, People and Ideas

10.	Force, Work and Energy	Force: types of force. Work: simple machines—lever, pulley, wheel and axle, inclined plane, screw and wedge. Energy: energy and its sources— solar, wind, water and geothermal. Different forms of energy.	Learns the different types of forces. Understands what is work and the different simple machines used to do work. Gains knowledge of energy and its sources. Learns the different forms of energy.	What makes the given toys move? Choose the correct option. Name the simple machines seen in the picture of a construction site. Draw a railway station and show different simple machines used in that place.

Unit 5: Natural Phenomena

11.	Air, Water and Weather	Air: atmosphere, wind, gale, storm, thunderstorm, breeze —land and sea breeze. Sun causes changes in weather, winds to blow, changes in states of water— evaporation and condensation. Water cycle. Weather and crops.	Lists the names of moving air depending on its speed. Understands that sun causes changes in weather. Realizes that proper weather is necessary for the growth of crops.	Complete the sentences by writing what you do on a hot, cold and rainy day. Experiment to show that sand becomes hotter and cooler faster than water. Experiment to show that water vapour condenses to form water. Experiment to show that liquid water changes to solid ice on freezing. Draw an object on each poster which depicts three types of weather on three different days. Show the journey of a water drop in the water cycle by drawing a series of pictures.

Unit 6: Natural Resources

12.	Soil	Soil formation. Types of soil — sandy, clayey, loam. Contents of soil. Soil and crops.	Learns how soil is formed. Understands that there are different types of soil and loam is good for growing plants. Gains knowledge about the contents of soil. the importance of soil. Realizes the importance of soil.	Identify the things which are made of clay and colour them brown. Experiment to see the different components of soil. Experiment to show that soil contains water. Experiment to show that soil contains air. Experiment to show that different type of soil lets different quantity of water to pass through. Label the given diagram. Interview a farmer. Observe the different types of soil and
13.	A Clean World	Pollution: air, water, land. Acid rain. Disposal of waste. Preventing pollution. Reduce, reuse, recycle.	Learns about pollution. Understands the importance of preventing pollution.	Unscramble the letters and write the correct words to show what you need to save for a clean world. Colour the biodegradable waste bin and the non-biodegradable waste bin with the suitable colours. Make a project on recycling centre.

Unit 7: Our Universe

14.	Our Earth and its Neighbours	The sun and the solar system. Artficial satellites. Our earth. Volcano. Movements of the earth. Day and night. Seasons.	Learns about the solar system. Realizes the importance of artificial satellites. Gains knowledge about the earth and its movements. Draws diagrams.	Find out the season during christmas in the northern hemisphere and in the southern hemisphere. Find out the names of five artificial satellites.

Preface

I Explore is an eight-level series of science textbooks for grades 1 to 8. As envisaged in the National Curriculum Framework (2005) guidelines, the *I Explore* books are designed to present science as a living body of knowledge where students are encouraged and guided to make exploratory forays of their own. Every effort has been made to extend learning beyond the classroom in a holistic manner.

Books 1 to 5 lay stress on learning with understanding. They comprehensively deal with all the elementary aspects of science, and help in forming basic ideas about nature and the immediate environment of a child. The books adopt a thematic and activity-oriented approach with a simple and clear style of presentation to make the understanding of science easy.

The books are full of exciting activities and simple experiments which will introduce young children to basic concepts of science.

The books are well-illustrated with numerous photographs, diagrams, tables, flowcharts, etc. These provide an appropriate method of communication and serve as an invaluable tool in shaping up the thinking and observational skills of children.

Each chapter begins with a *Warm Up* in which the children are expected to draw upon their existing knowledge. It provides the teacher with an insight into the knowledge and skills already possessed by each child. Scientific definitions are explained in a clear and simple language to build the foundation for further scientific study. The *Activities* in all the chapters are designed to develop students' skill of experimentation. Each chapter contains *Do you know?* which presents snippets of interesting information to take learning beyond the syllabus. *Now you know* in-text exercises are designed to ensure revision and reinforcement of the concepts learnt before moving on to the next section. *Points to Remember* are listed at the end of the chapters to recapitulate the important points learnt. Meanings of difficult words are given in *New Words* section at the end of each chapter.

The exercises have been designed to develop skills of creative and critical thinking by including questions based on *Higher Order Thinking Skills (HOTS)*. *Task* and *Brainstorm* sections have been designed to develop various co-scholastic skills. *Project Idea* section helps in fostering skills of investigation and experimentation.

Sample test papers have been given at the end of each book for self-assessment. Additional *teacher support* material are available at www.cambridgeindia.org.

The student's books are available both with CD-ROM and without CD-ROM.

A *Teacher's Manual* for each level gives necessary inputs to the teachers to help them develop the lessons.

It is hoped that the series will inculcate a spirit of scientific enquiry among the young learners.

Mrinalini Pradhan

[1] Our Food

Draw four different types of food you eat every day in the boxes below.

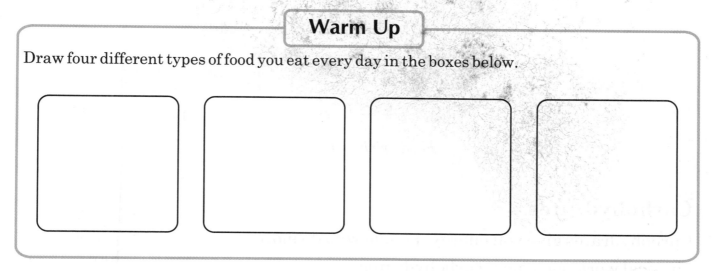

All living things need food. Food gives you energy to work. It helps you to grow and keep healthy. It also helps in repairing the wear and tear of your body.

When the food you eat is used up by your body, you feel hungry and weak.

Nutrients

Food contains different substances which are useful to your body. These substances are called **nutrients.** These nutrients are necessary for life and growth.

Food contains nutrients like **proteins**, **fats**, **carbohydrates, vitamins** and **minerals.** It also contains **water** and **roughage.**

We need food to live and grow

Proteins

Proteins help your body to grow. They help your body to build muscles, other organs and blood. That is why foods which contain proteins are called **body-building food.**

1

Proteins also help to repair the wear and tear of the body.

Children need more proteins than adults as they grow more rapidly than adults.

Meat, fish, eggs, milk, cheese, pulses and nuts are rich in proteins.

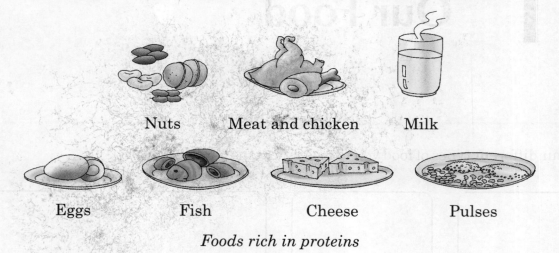

Foods rich in proteins

Carbohydrates

Carbohydrates give you energy. People who do more physical work need more carbohydrates.

Sugar and **starch** are two types of carbohydrates.

Rice, sugar and potatoes are some of the foods which are rich in carbohydrates.

Foods rich in carbohydrates

Fats

Fats too give you energy. They also help to keep your body warm.

Oil, butter, ghee, nuts and fish contain fats. Too much fat is not good for your health.

Foods rich in fats

Foods rich in carbohydrates and fats are called **energy- giving foods.**

Vitamins and minerals

Vitamins and minerals are needed in small amount by your body. They keep your body healthy. They also help your body to fight diseases. So they are called **protective foods.** You must have them every day.

Vitamins: There are different types of vitamins like Vitamin A, Vitamin B, Vitamin C, Vitamin D, Vitamin E and Vitamin K.

We need vitamins and minerals for good health

Minerals: There are many different minerals such as calcium and iron which are needed by your body. You need calcium for strong bones and teeth. Iron helps in the formation of blood.

Wheat, meat, egg, fish, milk, cheese, vegetables and fruits are rich in vitamins and minerals.

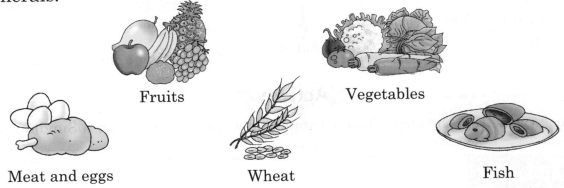

Fruits   Vegetables

Meat and eggs   Wheat   Fish

Foods rich in vitamins and minerals

Roughage and water

Roughage is the fibre part of the food we eat. It cannot be digested and also has no food value. But it is very important as it helps our body to move the undigested food through the digestive system and out of the body. Fruits and vegetables are rich in roughage.

3

Water is needed by our body to function properly. Food contains some amount of water. But it is not sufficient. Your body needs more water. You must drink at least four to five glasses of water every day.

We should drink plenty of water

Do you know?

Tomato, which is considered a vegetable, is actually a fruit. It is a fruit because it grows from a flower and has seeds inside it.

A Balanced Diet

The food you eat every day is your **diet**. The diet that provides all the nutrients in the right amount is a **balanced diet**. A balanced diet keeps you fit and healthy.

Scientists use a food pyramid which shows how much of different types of food you should eat in a day for a correct balanced diet.

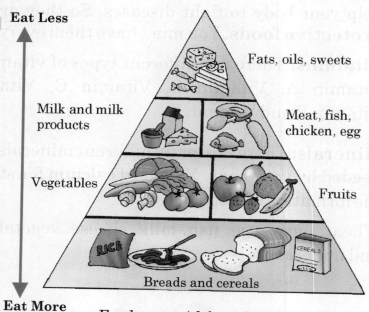

Food pyramid for a balanced diet

Activity

Select food types from the above food pyramid and write your menu for a Sunday.

Now you know

The nutrients required by our body are:

1. _____ .   2. _____ .
3. _____ .   4. _____ .
5. _____ .

4

Alertness Concerning Food

Cleaning the raw food

Fruits and vegetables are grown in fields. Very often, dust and mud stick to them. These dust and mud carry germs which cause diseases. Fruits and vegetables are also sprayed with chemicals to protect them from diseases. But these chemicals are harmful for us. Therefore, food should be washed thoroughly before eating. If fruits and vegetables are washed after they are cut, some of the nutrients are also washed away with water. So, they should always be washed before cutting.

Fruits and vegetables must be washed before cutting

Precautions while cooking

Fruits and some vegetables like carrots, cucumber and radish are eaten raw. But other foods have to be cooked before eating. Cooking makes the food soft, tasty and easy to digest. It also kills the germs. The different methods of cooking food are **boiling, steaming, frying, roasting, baking,** etc.

Rice: Boiled food

Idli: Steamed food

Puri: Fried food

Chicken: Roasted food

Bread: Baked food

Different methods of cooking food

Food should not be cooked for too long. If food is overcooked, a number of useful nutrients are destroyed.

Food should be cooked in just enough water. Extra water in cooked food also contains nutrients. If the extra water is thrown away, the nutrients in it are also lost.

Preserving food

Food gets spoilt if it is kept for a long time. Germs or moulds start growing in it. You fall ill if you eat such food. There are different methods to avoid rotting of food. This is called **preservation of food**. Preserved food remains good for a long time.

The different methods of preservation are **freezing**, **drying**, **canning**, and **adding salt, sugar, vinegar** or **oil**.

Sometimes artificial chemical substances called **preservatives** are added to the food.

Freezing

Drying

Canning

Adding sugar, salt or oil

Some methods of food preservation

Points to Remember

- Food is made up of different substances called nutrients which provide nourishment to our body.
- Food contains nutrients like proteins, fats, carbohydrates, vitamins and minerals. It also contains water and roughage.
- Fruits and vegetables should be washed thoroughly before eating.
- The different methods of cooking food are boiling, steaming, frying, roasting, baking, etc.
- Preserved food remains good for a longer time.

New Words

Nutrients: substances in food which provide nourishment to the body

Diet: the food and drink we take on a regular basis

Preservation: keeping something in a good condition for a long time

Canning: to keep food and drink in a closed container without water

A. Fill in the blanks with the correct option.

1. The nutrients that help your body to grow are _____ . vitamins/proteins

2. The nutrients present in large quantity in potatoes are _____ . carbohydrates/minerals

3. Body-building foods are rich in_____ . proteins/fats

4. If food is overcooked, useful _____ are lost. fuels/nutrients

5. _____ is a method of cooking food. Steaming/Freezing

B. Match the following.

1. fat	a. boiling
2. iron	b. preservation
3. starch	c. butter
4. cooking	d. mineral
5. canning	e. carbohydrate

C. Answer these questions.

1. What are nutrients?
2. Write two foods which are rich in carbohydrates.
3. Name any two minerals which are needed in small amounts by your body.
4. What is a balanced diet?
5. Why do we cook food?

D. Give reasons.

1. Proteins should be included in our daily diet.
2. Vitamins and minerals are called protective foods.
3. Fruits and vegetables should be washed before eating.
4. Food should be cooked in just enough water.

7

Task

Visit a market with your parents. Find out all the food items that are available. Think and tell your parents what food items to choose for the family and why?

Brainstorm

Discuss in your class the type of foods you should take regularly and the type of foods you should avoid.

Project Idea

Note down for a week what you eat in your meals. Note down the major nutrients these foods contain. Write if you think the food you ate for the week was balanced or not.

Unit 1: Food

[2] Teeth and Digestion

Warm Up

Write a caption and a slogan for the picture.

Caption: _____

Slogan: _____

Our Teeth

We all have a pair of jaws in our mouth. The upper jaw is fixed but the lower jaw can move. Each jaw has a row of hard, bone-like teeth. Together, they form a complete set of teeth.

How are teeth useful to us?

Teeth give proper shape to our face. They also help us to speak properly. But most importantly, teeth help us to chew our food. Chewing breaks down the food into smaller pieces so that they can be swallowed and digested easily.

Temporary teeth and permanent teeth

When a baby is born, its teeth are not seen. The baby has tooth buds inside the gums. The teeth start growing when the baby is about six months old. By the time the baby becomes three years old, it has a set of twenty teeth. This set of first teeth is called **temporary teeth** or **milk teeth**.

A six-month-old baby has temporary teeth

9

When a child is about six years old, the next set of teeth starts appearing. The second set of teeth is called **permanent teeth**. As the permanent teeth grow, they push the milk teeth out. Children have twenty-eight teeth.

At the age of about eighteen years, four more teeth start growing. These are called **wisdom teeth**. An adult has a full set of thirty-two teeth. Sixteen of these are on the upper jaw and sixteen on the lower jaw.

Children over six years have permanent teeth

Activity

Find out and note down the number of milk teeth and the number of permanent teeth each child in your class has.

Now you know

Fill in the blanks.

- Temporary teeth are also called _____ teeth.
- The second set of teeth is called _____ teeth.
- Number of teeth children have is _____.

Types of Teeth

All the teeth are not alike. They have different shapes. Their shape depends on their functions.

The four teeth at the front of each jaw are specially made for cutting the food. They are called **incisors.**

There are two pointed teeth, one on each side of the incisors. Their work is to grip and tear the food. They are called **canines.**

The remaining teeth are flat, grinding and chewing teeth. They are called **premolars** and **molars**. There are four **premolars**—two

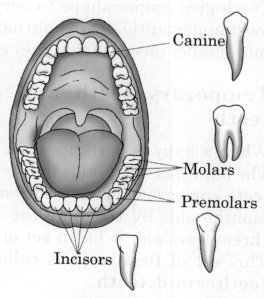

Types of teeth

on each side of a jaw. Behind these are the **molars** which are broader than the premolars. There are six molars in each jaw— three on each side.

Now you know

Match the following.

1. incisors   a. grip and tear
2. canines   b. grind and chew
3. molars   c. cutting

The Structure of a Tooth

Teeth are fixed in the soft gums of the jaw. The part of a tooth which is outside the gum is known as the **crown**, while the part which is inside the gum is known as the **root**. The **neck** of the tooth is where the crown meets the root.

Gums protect the bottom of the tooth, including the root.

The outer white part of the tooth is known as **enamel**. It is also the hardest part of the body. **Dentine** is the next layer of our tooth. It is tough, but not as much as the enamel. The **pulp** is the innermost layer of the tooth. It has blood vessels and nerves.

Root is the sensory portion of the tooth, containing the nerve which leads to the brain. The root also holds the tooth in place in the jawbone.

11

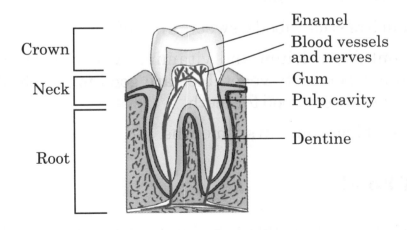

The structure of a tooth

Care of Teeth

Many types of **germs** live in the mouth. Germs are tiny living things which cause diseases. They feed on the leftover food particles and give out a substance called

acid. The acid damages the enamel. Slowly a hole called **cavity** is formed. The hole gets deeper in the tooth and reaches the dentine and then the pulp. The nerves in the soft pulp begin to pain. Then it is difficult to chew the food. This causes indigestion.

Cavities cause pain, bad breath and indigestion. A visit to the dentist becomes necessary in such cases. A **dentist** is a doctor who looks after your teeth.

Our permanent teeth have to last a life time. If they are damaged or lost, they do not grow again. So, we must take good care of our teeth.

Brush your teeth correctly and properly as shown in the pictures below.

Toothache is painful

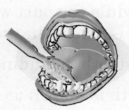

Outside:Brush in circles and up and down

Inside:Brush up and down

Top:Brush back and forth

- Do not forget to clean your tongue properly.
- Rinse your mouth after every meal.
- Do not eat too much of sticky foods, sweets and soft drinks.
- Eat food that contains calcium and vitamins A, C and D. Foods like milk, cheese, fruits and green leafy vegetables are good for teeth. Apples and raw carrots are considered very good for teeth.
- Visit your dentist at least once in six months.

Digestion of Food

The food we eat is used by our body to get energy to do work and also for growth. But the food we eat cannot be used as it is. It has to be broken down into very simple soluble forms. This simple food can then dissolve in the blood and be carried to all parts of our body. This process of breaking down of food into simpler form is called **digestion.** Organs which help in digesting food are called **digestive organs.**

Take two glasses. Fill them with water. Add one teaspoon of wheat flour to one glass and one teaspoon of sugar to the other glass. Stir the water in both the glasses. You will notice that wheat flour does not dissolve in water, but the sugar does. It is because sugar is soluble in water, but wheat flour is insoluble in water.

Sugar   Wheat flour

Similarly, the food that we eat does not dissolve in the blood directly. The starch in the rice or wheat changes into sugar during digestion. The sugar dissolves in the blood.

The process of digestion

Food is digested in the **alimentary canal**. The alimentary canal consists of the food pipe or the **oesophagus**, the **stomach**, the **small intestine** and the **large intestine**.

In the mouth: The process of digestion begins in the mouth. Our **teeth** chew the food and break it into very small pieces.

13

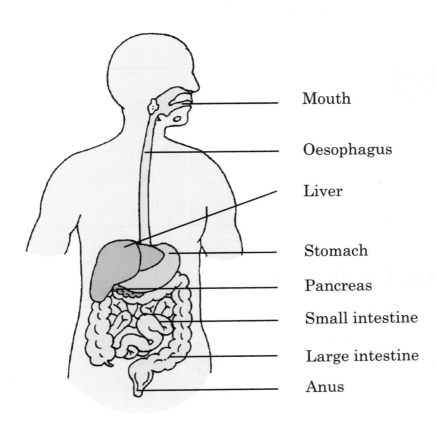

Mouth

Oesophagus

Liver

Stomach

Pancreas

Small intestine

Large intestine

Anus

Digestive system

As we chew, the **saliva** in our mouth mixes with the food. Saliva is a digestive juice produced by salivary glands in the mouth. The saliva converts insoluble starch into soluble sugar.

In the stomach: The food now enters the alimentary canal. It passes through the oesophagus to the stomach. The stomach is a muscular bag. In the stomach, the food is churned and digestive juices are added. The food turns into a semi-liquid mixture. Here the proteins are broken into simpler form.

In the small intestine: The mixture is pushed gradually into a long, coiled tube called the small intestine. Some juices secreted by the small intestine are added to the mixture.

The digestive juices from the **liver** and the **pancreas** enter the small intestine and are added to the food mixture. The liver makes a digestive juice called **bile**. Bile helps to digest fats. The action of all these juices converts the food into different soluble substances.

The blood vessels present in the walls of the small intestine absorb the soluble substances into the blood. The blood carries these to all the parts of the body.

In the large intestine: The undigested food passes into another tube called the large intestine. Here, water is absorbed from the undigested food. Whatever is left over is thrown out of the body through an opening called **anus.**

Now you know

Fill in the blanks.

- Food passes from oesophagus to the_____.
- Bile is produced by the _____.
- Saliva is produced by the _____ glands.

Good Eating Habits

- Eat a balanced diet.
- Eat your food at fixed times.
- Chew your food well. Do not be in a hurry.
- Do not play as soon as you finish eating.
- Do not overeat.

Eat your food at fixed times

Do you know?

Our body uses whatever food is needed. The extra food turns into fat and is stored in the body. Gathering extra fat makes one overweight and obese. So, you must not overeat.

Points to Remember

- We have two sets of teeth in our life time—milk teeth (20 in number) and permanent teeth (32 in number).
- We have four types of teeth—*incisors* for cutting, *canines* for gripping and tearing, and *premolars* and *molars* for grinding and chewing the food.
- Enamel, dentine and pulp are the three layers of the tooth.
- We should take care of our teeth.
- The process of breaking down of food into simpler form is called digestion.
- The process of digestion begins in the mouth.
- Food is digested in the alimentary canal.

New Words

Incisors: cutting teeth

Canines: teeth which grip and tear

Molars: grinding and chewing teeth

Soluble: able to be dissolved or mix completely with a liquid

Insoluble: impossible to dissolve in a liquid

Oesophagus: food pipe

Digestion: process of breaking down of food into simpler form

Obese: very fat

15

Exercises

A. Fill in the blanks with the correct option.

1. Number of teeth in a complete set of permanent teeth is _____. 20/32

2. Teeth used for chewing and grinding are _____. canines/molars

3. The _____ is the innermost layer of the tooth. pulp/enamel

4. In the mouth, the food mixes with _____. acid/saliva

5. The bile from the liver mixes with the food in the _____.
   stomach/small intestine

B. **Correct the following sentences.**
   1. A small baby has tooth buds inside the tongue.
   2. The colour of teeth depends on their function.
   3. The outermost part of the tooth is called dentine.
   4. Saliva helps in the digestion of protein.
   5. Bile helps to digest carbohydrates.
   6. Water is absorbed in the small intestine.

C. **Match the following.**

1.	incisor	a.	food pipe
2.	mouth	b.	bile
3.	small intestine	c.	teeth
4.	oesophagus	d.	saliva
5.	liver	e.	long coiled tube

16

D. **Answer these questions.**
   1. Name the different types of teeth and their functions.
   2. Draw and label the structure of a tooth.
   3. What causes tooth decay?
   4. How should you take care of your teeth?
   5. What is meant by digestion of food?
   6. Draw a diagram and write what happens to the food in the stomach.
   7. What is the main role of the large intestine?

Task

Draw a diagram of the alimentary canal and label its parts.

Brainstorm

Make a banner showing how to take care of teeth and write a jingle next to it.

Project Idea

Visit a dentist's clinic. Observe the different types of tooth problems with which patients come to the dentist. Record the type of treatment prescribed by the dentist for these dental problems.

Unit 2: Materials

[3] Safety

Which safety equipment do they all have in common? Name it and draw one in the box.

Accidents always happen all of a sudden. They cause a lot of pain and suffering. Sometimes they can cause serious injuries or even loss of life.

You should always be careful and try to avoid accidents at home and outside by following some important safety rules.

Safety at Home

Do not play with sharp or pointed objects. You might cut yourself and suffer from blood loss.

Do not leave your toys on the floor. Keep them in their proper place after you finish playing. Otherwise, you may trip over them.

Do not climb on shelves, windows, tables, etc.

Be careful of slippery floors.

Do not play with breakable things like glass. You may get hurt.

Some chemicals are harmful even if you touch them. Be careful.

Medicines should be taken only in the presence of an adult.

Do not play with electrical appliances. Do not touch electric wires or switches with wet hands. You might get a shock.

Do not play near gas stoves, hot pots and pans. Burns are very painful.

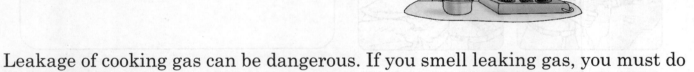

Leakage of cooking gas can be dangerous. If you smell leaking gas, you must do the following:

- Open all the windows and the doors for the gas to escape.

- Turn off the regulator of the gas cylinder.

- Do not touch any switch. Even a small spark is enough to catch fire.

- Do not light a matchstick. The gas in the room will catch fire. Contact the gas agency immediately.

Safety at School

In school, you run around a lot. You also do a lot of work using sharp tools like pens, pencils and scissors. A few precautions can take care of some unwanted incidents.

- Do not push each other.

- Do not run while climbing or going down the staircase.

- Be careful while handling sharp or pointed objects. You might hurt yourself or others.

- Do not play in the classroom.

- Do not climb on the desks. You may hurt yourself.

- Do not fight with your friends.

Safety on the Playground

- Be careful while playing on the swings, slides and jungle gym.

- Do not push others. Wait for your turn.

- Do not push vacant swings.

- Do not go too close to the moving swings.

- Follow the rules of the game. Do not use sports equipment to hurt others.

Write 'Yes' for what you should do and 'No' for what you should not do.

- Play with a knife. _____
- Wait for your turn on the swings. _____
- Light a matchstick to check cooking gas leakage. _____
- Take medicines on your own. _____

Safety on Road

Do not walk on the road. Use the footpath to walk. If there is no raised footpath, walk on the right side so that you can see the traffic coming towards you.

20

Be careful while crossing the road. Use the zebra crossing wherever it is available.

Look first to your right and then to the left to see if any vehicle is coming. Cross the road only after you are sure that the road is clear.

Do not play or run on the road.   Wear proper shoes.

Follow traffic rules when you ride your bicycle on the road. Do not forget to wear your helmet.

Do not listen to music with a headphone while riding on your bicycle. It can keep you from hearing the sound or horn of a moving vehicle.

Be careful if the road is wet. Vehicles may skid on wet or oil spilled roads.

Activity

Prepare a chart on road safety and display it in your class.

Rail Safety Tips

Do not stand near the door of the moving train.

Wait for the train to stop before getting in or out of the train.

Do not walk on the tracks or in the tunnels.

Do not place any object on the tracks. They can become dangerous missiles and hurt people nearby.

Do not throw any object at the train. It can hurt people on the train or even you.

Cross the railway tracks only at the railway crossing or use the foot over bridge.

While crossing the railway tracks at the gate, wait for the gates to open. Going around lowered gates is dangerous.

First Aid

Whenever a person is hurt, the first medical help the person gets is called **first aid.** Your school must have a first-aid box. We should always have a first-aid box at home for any immediate need.

First-aid box

A first-aid box usually has the following things:

- a first-aid book
- small pieces of clean cloth
- a crepe bandage
- a pair of forceps (tweezers)
- a pencil torch
- a small roll of sterilized gauge and cotton pads

- a small cotton roll
- some Band-aid
- a pair of scissors
- a thermometer
- a small soap

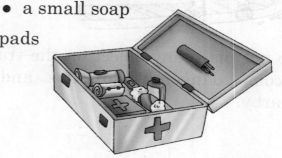

Medicines in a first-aid box

- an antiseptic lotion to clean wounds
- an antiseptic cream to apply on cuts and wounds
- an anti-burn cream

If somebody gets hurt, the wound should always be cleaned before applying an antiseptic cream. An antiseptic prevents infection caused by germs.

An antiseptic cream can also be applied for an insect bite.

For minor burns, pour cold water on that part and then apply medicine.

A wound should never be ignored. If the wound is deep, you should give first aid to the person only if you are trained for it. Otherwise, he should be taken to a doctor as early as possible.

Points to Remember

- Accidents cause a lot of harm, pain and suffering.
- You must follow safety rules at all times to avoid accidents.
- At home be careful with sharp and pointed tools, electrical appliances, heaters and stoves, slippery floors, medicines, etc.
- In school, take care not to jump around and push others.
- On the playground or park, use the game equipment carefully.
- Be watchful on the road and near railway tracks.
- Always keep a first-aid box at home.

 ## New Words

Equipment: anything made for a particular use

Electrical appliance: an object which runs on electricity

Skid: to suddenly slip or slide sideways

Missile: an object or weapon that can travel a long way

Sterilized: made free of germs

Antiseptic: medicine which prevents growth of germs

Exercises

A. Fill in the blanks with the correct option.

1. You must follow _____ rules to avoid accidents. school/safety

2. Some_____ are harmful even if you touch them. chemicals/clothes

3. If the gas from a cooking gas cylinder leaks, you must_____the windows and doors. open/close

4. You must not play with _____ objects. soft/sharp

5. Always use the _____ while walking on the road. footpath/road

6. Do not_____ at the door of a moving train. look/stand

B. Complete the following sentences.

1. You must not leave your toys on the floor because

_____

_____

2. You must not play in the classroom because

_____

_____

3. While riding a bicycle, you should be careful if the road is wet because

_____

_____

4. You must not throw any object at the train because

_____

_____

5. The wound should always be cleaned before applying an antiseptic because

_____

_____

C. Answer these questions.

1. What precautions will you take to avoid falling down at home?

24

2. What will you do if the cooking gas cylinder starts leaking?
3. Why should you not listen to music while riding a bicycle?
4. What safety rules should you follow before crossing the road?
5. What rules should you follow while crossing the railway tracks?
6. What should you do if somebody gets a minor burn on the hand?

Task

Stand at the window for 15 minutes and note down how many people ride on two wheelers without wearing a helmet.

Brainstorm

Read the newspaper for a week and note down how many accidents have occurred due to carelessness. Think and discuss how they could have been avoided.

Project Idea

Prepare a project on the different road traffic symbols used in a city to prevent road accidents.

Unit 2: Materials

[4] Clothes and Fibres

Look at the picture and tick (✓) mark the things which are made of cloth.

As you can see from the picture, we use clothes in many different ways.

We need clothes for wearing. We need clothes to furnish our homes. We need clothes to make bags and covers. We need clothes for many other things. Clothes are an important part of our day-to-day life.

Clothes are made from long, thin strands or threads of material called **fibres**. These fibres are put together by various processes to make broad spreads of clothes or **fabrics.**

Fibre

Fabrics

Sources of Fibres

We get fibres from natural as well as artificial sources. Fibres that we get from plants and animals are called **natural fibres**. We also produce fibres from different chemicals in factories. These are called **synthetic fibres**.

Natural Fibres

Plant fibres

Cotton: The cotton plant bears light and fluffy cotton bolls which burst open. These cotton bolls have thin fibres in them.

Cotton plant

Linen: Linen fibre is produced from the stalk of the flax plant. The stems of flax plants are allowed to rot. Then they are beaten to separate the long fibres. These fibres are woven into **linen** cloth.

The fibres are twisted or **spun** into strong threads called **yarn**. Spinning is done with a spinning wheel or with spinning machines.

A wooden spinning wheel   A modern spinning machine

Do you know?

Around 25 million tonnes of cotton are produced each year worldwide. China, United States, Pakistan, India, Uzbekistan, Turkey and Brazil are the major producers of cotton.

27

The yarn is later woven together on a machine called a **loom** to make cloth.

A traditional hand loom

A modern power loom

Sometime the cloth is dyed with colours or printed after that.

Clothes being dyed

Clothes being printed with wooden blocks

Cotton and linen are mostly used in making clothes for wearing.

Jute: Jute fibre is produced from the stem and outer skin of the jute plant. **Hessian,** the thick rough cloth made from jute, is mostly used in making sacks, bags, curtains, carpets, rugs and ropes.

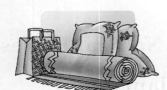
Jute products

Coir: Coir is produced from the outer shell of a coconut. Coir is used to make doormats, mattresses, brushes, sacks and ropes.

Coir products

Now you know

Fill in the blanks.

- Fibres obtained from plant and animal sources are called _____ fibres.
- Fibres obtained from chemicals are called _____ fibres.
- A _____ is used to weave yarn into cloth.

Animal fibres

Wool: Animals that have a thick coat of hair on their skin give us wool. The coat is called **fleece**. We get wool mostly from sheep. We also get some wool from goats and camels. The fleece is cut off or **sheared**. It has fibres.

Woollen fibres are made into woollen threads and then woven into woollen cloth.

Woollen cloth is used to make warm clothes like coats, jackets and blankets.

Wool that has been moistened, pressed together and allowed to shrink into a thick flat sheet is known as **felt**. Felt is often used in industry and musical instruments to reduce the effect of vibrations.

Woollen yarn is also used to knit different clothes like sweaters, gloves and socks.

Woollen clothes keep us warm. So they are used in winter. They don't crush easily.

A sheep being sheared

A sweater being knitted

Silk: Silk fibres are made by an insect called **silk moth**. Silk moths lay eggs. The eggs hatch into caterpillars or silkworms. Young silkworms eat mulberry leaves and grow. The silkworms spin a silky thread and wrap it around their bodies. This silky covering is called a **cocoon**. The cocoons are put in hot water and then skilled workers carefully unwind this thread. The thread is woven into a silk cloth.

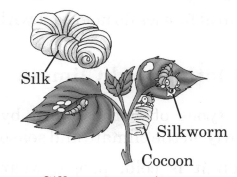
Silkworm growing on mulberry leaves

The soft touch and shiny look of silk makes it an important fibre to make expensive clothes, furnishings and carpets.

Now you know

Write one or two words for the following.

- Cutting of fleece   :   _____
- Insect which makes silk fibre   :   _____
- Food of silkworms   :   _____

Synthetic Fibres

Fibres produced by chemical processes in factories are called synthetic fibres. Rayon, nylon, polyester, acrylic and terylene are some synthetic fibres.

Fabrics made out of synthetic fibres are used for similar purposes as natural clothes.

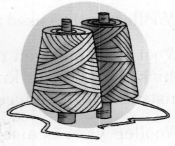

Do you know?

- Rayon was the first synthetic fibre developed.
- The word Nylon has been taken out of the name of two cities 'NY' from New York and 'LON' from London.

Differences between natural and synthetic fabrics

Synthetic fabrics are stronger than natural fibre and are more durable.

Natural fibres like cotton and linen do not catch fire easily. But synthetic clothes catch fire easily. They should not be worn while bursting crackers or cooking. They melt if touched by hot iron.

Cotton and linen clothes take time to dry. They also shrink a little and wrinkle easily. Synthetic fabrics dry quickly, do not shrink and need very little ironing.

Natural fabrics do not react with skin. But synthetic fabrics can cause rashes.

Clothes and Climate

The types of clothes worn by people depend greatly on the climate and season of that area.

When it is cold, people wear heavy woollen garments to protect themselves from cold. They also wear shoes, socks and gloves.

When it is warm, people use clothes made of cotton and linen. These clothes are light and have pores that absorb sweat. This allows our body heat to escape and makes us feel cool and comfortable.

Points to Remember

- Fibre is a long, thin strand or thread of material.
- Cloth is made by weaving or knitting threads together.
- Fibres that we get from plants and animals are called natural fibres.
- Man-made fibres are known as synthetic fibres.
- The fibres are twisted or spun into yarn and later woven together to make cloth.
- Wool is obtained from fleece of some animals.
- Silk fibres are collected from the cocoons of silkworm.
- Clothes worn by people depend on the climate.

 ## New Words

Furnish: to have furniture

Fibre: long, thin strand or thread of material

Loom: weaving machine

Dyed: coloured

Fleece: coat of an animal

Shear: to cut off or trim the fleece

Knit: to make a fabric by joining together pieces of heavy threads by hand with long needles or by machines

Cocoon: silky covering spun by the silkworm

Wrinkle: a fold on a cloth

 ## Exercises

A. Fill in the blanks with the correct option.

1. Clothes are made from long, thin strands or threads of material called _____ . fabrics/fibres

2. Fibres are_____ into threads. knit/spun

3. Warm clothes are made from _____ fibres. woollen/linen

4. _____ is obtained from coconut fibres. Jute/Coir

5. _____ cloth is used for making sacks. Hessian/Silk

B. Match the following.

1. fleece
2. cocoon
3. loom
4. linen
5. rubber

a. weaving machine
b. coat of sheep
c. flax
d. silkworm
e. waterproof

C. Answer these questions.

1. How do you get coloured, printed cotton cloth?
2. How do we get wool?
3. How is silk cloth made?
4. How do we get fibres from flax plant?
5. What are the differences between natural fibres and synthetic fibres?

Task

Divide the class into two groups. The first group acts out as manufacturers of natural fibres and the second group acts out as manufacturers of synthetic fibres. Let each group put together a presentation to convince others that their fibres are superior and should be preferred to the fibres of the other group.

Brainstorm

Find out and write down the differences between the type of clothes a farmer wears and a factory worker wears.

Project Idea

In your scrapbook, paste photographs of the type of clothes you wear at home, while playing, in school and when you attend a wedding. Write the name of each dress.

Unit 2: Materials

[5] Houses All Around

Warm Up

Name the persons who use these tools while building a house.

_____   _____   _____   _____

How many different types of houses have you seen? Houses can be big or small. Houses may have sloping roofs or flat roofs. Roofs of houses may be made of straw, leaves, tiles, tin sheets or cement. Houses may have walls built of mud, stones, wood or bricks. The doors and windows may be built of wood, steel or glass.

A small house with a sloping roof

A multistoried building

Tent

The type of houses built in a place depends on the climate of that place, building materials available in the place and the money available with a person to build a house.

Climate

Climate is the usual weather condition in a place. It plays an important role on the types of houses seen in a place.

A mud house

Mud and clay houses with a thatched roof remain cool in summer and warm in winter. This type of houses is found in small towns which have very hot or very cold climate. Thick walls keep the house cool. So, in hot places houses are built with thick walls.

Places which receive a lot of rainfall have houses built on **stilts** to avoid rain water from entering inside. These houses also have sloping roofs for the rain water to flow down without affecting the house.

A stilt house

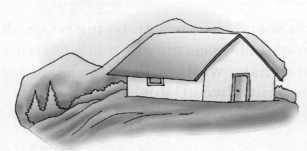

A house with sloping roofs

Houses on hills also have sloping roofs for rain water and snow to slide off easily without damaging the roofs.

Building Materials

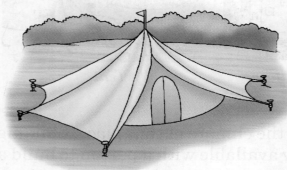

A tent

Building materials are the materials used for construction.

There are two types of building materials— natural and synthetic.

Fabric is used to make tents. Natural as well as synthetic fibres are used.

Low-cost houses are often built with natural materials which are locally available and do not cost much.

These houses are small and usually built with **mud, clay, sand, gravel** and **straw.** Some houses are built with **branches, twigs, leaves** and **bark** of trees.

Low-cost housing materials

Igloo

In the icy lands of Greenland and other Arctic regions, Eskimos use ice blocks to build snow houses called igloos.

But these low-cost houses are temporary and need repairs very often. To make houses that are big and strong, and can last for many years, a number of other building materials are used.

Rocks such as sandstone and marble have been used for many years as a building material. They are known for their strength and long lasting quality. **Granite** is widely used in construction of floors and **slate** is used as roofing material.

Granite slab

Slate roofing

Marble floor

Sandstone building

Wooden planks

Wood is used for making beams, planks, doors, windows, etc. Wood is useful in all types of climates.

Cement is mostly used to hold stone and brick walls together. **Concrete** is used because of its strength and long life.

Metals like steel and iron are used to make strong buildings. These are also used for grills and gates.

Glass is used in doors and windows because of its ability to let light in while keeping dust and insects away.

Plastic or **synthetic material** which can be easily moulded is used for making pipes, doors, windows, etc. These are waterproof and do not rust.

These materials are more expensive than locally available materials and, therefore, the houses made of these materials cost a lot of money.

Concrete and metal are used for their strength

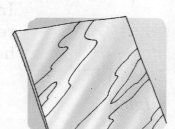

Glass is used in doors and windows

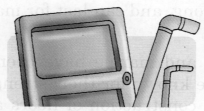

Plastic door and pipes

Budget

The money needed to build a house has to be considered before building a house. The amount of money fixed for building a house is known as its budget. The cost of a house depends on its size, building materials used, interior decoration of the house, cost of land, location, facilities available, etc.

Now you know

Fill in the blanks.

- Houses are built on stilts to avoid rain water from _____.
- There are two types of building materials: _____ and _____.
- Ice is used by _____ to build igloos.

36

People Who Build a House

A number of people with special skills are needed in the making of a big house.

The **architect** makes the plan or design of the house.

The **engineer** looks after the actual construction of the house.

The **mason** or bricklayer joins the bricks with mortar. The walls have to be strong and plastered.

The **carpenter** makes the doors, window frames, cupboards, etc.

The **fabricator** fixes iron grills and fences for security.

Architect

Engineer

Mason

Carpenter

Fabricator

37

Do you know?

Oxy-acetylene flame is used to join two materials by welding them together. This flame can also heat, cut and solder. It gives out a lot of heat and throws off sparks. Gloves and shaded eye protection and cotton clothes have to be used for protection.

The water pipes and sanitary wares, etc. are fixed by a **plumber**. The electricity connection is taken care of by **electricians**. Tiles are fixed by a **tiler**. The house is painted by the **painters** and decorated from inside and outside.

Plumber

Painter

Electrician

Tiler

If there is space, a garden is made by the **gardener**.

The house should have a proper drainage system and overhead tanks to store enough water.

Care of the house should be taken once it is built. It should be maintained properly. A neat and clean house ensures good health.

Gardener

Points to Remember

- Types of houses built in a place depend on the climate of that place, building materials used and budget.
- Building materials range from naturally available earth, wood, leaves and rocks to man-made cement, steel, plastic and glass.
- Budget or money needed has to be considered for building a house.
- Many people—architects, engineers, masons, carpenters, electricians, etc. put in efforts to build a proper house.
- Care of the house should be taken once it is built.

New Words

Climate: the usual weather conditions in a place

Stilts: long poles used to support a structure built above the surface of water or land

Concrete: a very hard building material made by mixing together cement, sand, small stones and water

Grill: a frame of metal bars used as a screen or barrier

Rust: a red or brown substance that forms on the surface of some metals when they come in contact with water

Budget: plan for using money

Architect: the person who designs a house

Engineer: the person who constructs the house

Fabricator: the person who makes and fixes metal grills, gates, etc.

Welding: to join metals by using heat

Solder: to use a melted mixture of metals to connect

Exercises

A. Fill in the blanks with the correct option.

1. _____ walls keep the house cool. Thick/Thin

2. _____ is used to make tents. Fabric/Clay

3. Ice is used to make _____. tents/igloos

4. Slate is used as _____ material. wall/roofing

5. Budget is the amount of _____ that has to be considered for building a house. land/money

B. Complete the following.

1. The types of houses built in an area depend on _____

   _____.

2. Concrete is used because of _____

   _____.

3. Metals like steel and iron are used to make _____

   _____.

4. The cost of a house depends on _____

   _____.

5. A house should have overhead tanks to _____

   _____.

C. Answer these questions in detail.

1. What are the advantages of having a thatched roof?

2. Name any five building materials used in making a low-cost, temporary house.

3. Name any five building materials used in making a big, permanent house.

4. Why is glass used as a building material?

5. Name the various people who work to build a house.

Task

Find the names of the following people in the wordsearch.

- MASON • ARCHITECT • ELECTRICIAN • CARPENTER
- PLUMBER • ENGINEER • TILER

M	T	C	A	R	P	E	N	T	E	R
P	L	T	C	V	O	N	X	L	C	K
U	P	K	M	G	P	G	C	Q	M	R
E	L	E	C	T	R	I	C	I	A	N
R	U	W	O	U	Z	N	K	N	S	S
C	M	B	T	I	L	E	R	L	O	J
N	B	T	G	P	F	E	R	V	N	S
T	E	H	C	Q	W	R	U	I	T	M
A	R	C	H	I	T	E	C	T	X	E

40

Brainstorm

Have you seen people who do not have a proper house to live in? Find out their living conditions.

Project Idea

1. Design and draw the house you would like to live in.
2. Make a model of a house using different types of materials.

Unit 2: Materials

[6] Solids, Liquids and Gases

Warm Up

What materials do you think the following things are made of?

Mirror

Table tennis ball

Utensils

Furniture

_____   _____   _____   _____

Look around your study table. You can see things made of different materials. You can see things made of wood, metal, plastic, glass, etc. All these materials are given a common name called **matter**.

Matter

All substances contain matter. The amount of matter in a substance is measured by its **weight**. Matter takes up some **space** to make a substance. The amount of space taken up by the matter of a substance is known as its **volume**. So anything which has weight and occupies space is called **matter**.

States of Matter

Matter is made of very tiny particles called **molecules**. They are so small that they cannot be seen. Depending on how the molecules are placed in a substance, the substance can be a solid, a liquid or a gas. These are the three states of matter.

Solids

In solids, the molecules are very closely packed. They do not have space between them to move. That is why solids have a definite shape, size and volume.

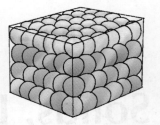
Molecules in a soild

Solids

Solids could be hard or soft. The shape of some solids can be changed by applying force. For example, a metal wire can be bent by twisting or can be flattened into a sheet by hitting it with a hammer. Some solids do not bend. They break into smaller pieces when force is applied on them, e.g. glass.

Now you know

Pictures of some solids are given below. Write **H** for the solids which are hard and **S** for the solids which are soft.

Liquids

In liquids, the molecules are not very closely packed. There is some space between the molecules. This allows the molecules some movement. That is why liquids do not have a definite shape.

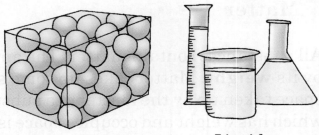
Molecules in a liquid   *Liquids*

Liquids flow when they are left on a flat surface. That is why liquids are also called **fluids**. Liquids flow from a higher level to a lower level. So liquids are kept in a vessel. They take the shape of the vessel in which they are kept.

Liquids have a definite volume. So the amount of liquid remains same even if it takes the shape of the container.

Take a glass of water and put a mark on the glass to show the water level. Pour the water carefully into a bottle such that no water spills out. You can see that the water has taken the shape of the bottle. Now pour the water back into the glass. Where is the water level in the glass? You will see that the water level touches the mark you had put earlier. So the volume of water did not change. This shows that liquids have definite volume.

Put a mark at the water level *Pour the water into the bottle* *Pour back the water in the glass* *Water level remains the same in the glass*

Gas

Molecules in a gas are placed far apart from each other. There is a lot of space between them. So, they can freely move about in any direction.

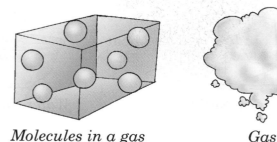

Molecules in a gas *Gas*

Hence, gases do not have a definite shape, nor do they have a definite volume. They take up all the space around. So gases have to be kept in closed containers.

43

Burn some coconut fibre or dry leaves to create a smoke. Hold a glass jar face down over it. As soon as some smoke enters the jar, cover the mouth of the jar with a lid. Place the jar on the table. What do you see? Is the gas seen only at one part of the jar or is it distributed evenly throughout the jar? Now open the lid. Does the smoke remain inside the jar? It flies away, showing that gases take up all the space available to them.

States of Matter are Interchangeable

You already know that water can exist in all the three states of matter. In normal conditions, water exists in its **liquid** state. But when it is heated, it becomes water vapour and exists in its **gaseous** state. When it is cooled, it becomes ice and exists in its **solid** state.

44

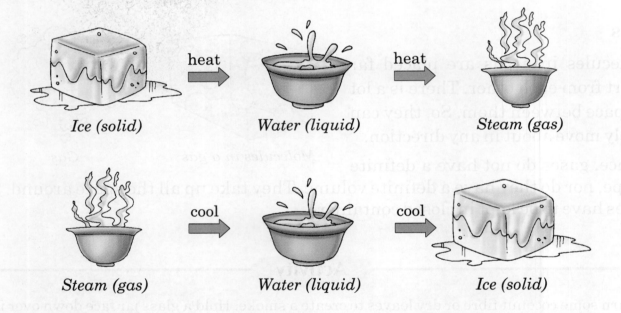

Ice (solid) → heat → Water (liquid) → heat → Steam (gas)

Steam (gas) → cool → Water (liquid) → cool → Ice (solid)

Like water, most other substances too change their state when they are heated or cooled. But the temperature at which they change their state is different for different substances.

Solids, liquids and gases are interchangeable states of matter.

When a solid is heated, its molecules loosen up. It melts and changes into a liquid. This process is called **melting**.

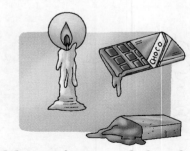

Melting of wax and chocolate

When a liquid is heated, the molecules become free. The liquid changes into its gas or vapour state. This process is called **evaporation**.

Evaporation of water

Water vapour condensed as water droplets

When a gas is cooled, its molecules condense or come closer. The gas changes back into liquid. This process is called **condensation.**

When a liquid is cooled, its molecules come even closer. They freeze into a close pack and turn into solid. This process is called **freezing.**

Water freezing into ice

Solubility

Activity

Take a glass of water. Add two teaspoons of sugar and stir. You will notice that the sugar disappears. If you taste the water, it will be sweet. This shows that the sugar has not vanished. It cannot be seen because it has completely mixed with the water. We say that the sugar has dissolved in the water.

When a liquid dissolves a solid substance in it, it is called a **solution**. The solid substance which dissolves in liquid is called a **solute,** and the liquid is called a **solvent.** In the above activity, sugar is the solute, water is the solvent and the sweet water is the solution.

The ability of a **solute** to dissolve in a solvent is known as its **solubility**.

Water is known as the **universal solvent** because it can dissolve a wide variety of substances. Substances that dissolve in water are **soluble** in it, while those that do not are **insoluble** in it.

Activity

Take a glass of water. Add two teaspoons of sand and stir. Observe what happens. You will notice that sand does not dissolve in water. It means sand is insoluble in water.

Do you know?

Have you seen that when the lid of the bottle or can of an aerated soft drink is opened, gas comes out in the form of bubbles? It is because carbon dioxide gas is dissolved in these cold drinks.

Activity

Take a glass of water. Put a mark on the water level. Now add two spoonfuls of sugar. Stir till the sugar dissolves. Measure the amount of solution formed.

You will notice that the water level in the glass has not gone up even after adding sugar to it. Water is a liquid. Therefore the molecules are loosely packed and there is space between the molecules. The sugar takes up that space. Hence, the volume of the solution does not increase when the sugar dissolves completely in the water.

Now you know

Fill in the blanks.

- State of water changes on _____ or _____.
- Substances which do not dissolve in a liquid are _____ in it.
- Solute and solvent together combine to form a _____.

New Words

Matter: something which has weight and occupies space

Molecules: tiny particles that make up matter

Interchangeable: able to be exchanged with each other

Soluble: that can be dissolved

Insoluble: that cannot be dissolved

Solute: a solid that is dissolved

Solvent: a liquid that is able to dissolve

Solution: mixture of a solute and a solvent

 **Exercises**

A. Fill in the blanks with the correct option.

1. Matter is made of tiny particles called _____.
   solutes/molecules

2. _____ flow from a higher level to a lower level. Solids/Liquids

3. States of matter are _____. fixed/interchangeable

4. _____ is known as the universal solvent. Oil/Water

5. In a sugar solution, sugar is the _____ . solute/solvent

47

B. State whether the following sentences are true or false.

1. Molecules are so small that they cannot be seen. _____

2. Gases have a definite shape and size. _____

3. On cooling, the gaseous state of water changes into its liquid state. _____

4. Sand is soluble in water. _____

5. The volume of a solution does not change if the solute completely dissolves in the solvent. _____

C. Answer these questions in a sentence.

1. What is matter?

2. Why do solids have a definite shape and size?

3. How is a gas able to spread in all directions?

4. Do molecules in a liquid have more space between them than solids?

5. What is solubility?

D. Answer these questions.

1. Draw diagrams showing the arrangement of molecules in solids, liquids and gases.

2. Write the differences between solids and liquids.

3. How can you change ice into steam?

Task

Testing solubility

Materials needed: A jug full of water, five glasses, a teaspoon, and two teaspoons each of salt, tea leaves, coffee powder, wheat flour and milk powder.

Method: Take the glasses. Add water from the jug in the glasses till they are half full. In each glass, add one teaspoonful of each of the ingredients and stir with the teaspoon. Observe and write which ingredient dissolved and which did not.

48

Brainstorm

Find out how we use the property of interchangeable states of matter in our daily life.

Project Idea

Prepare lemon juice and write about the solubility of sugar, salt and lemon juice in water.

Note down the things you used.

What did you do?

What happened?

What did this tell you?

Unit 3: The World of the Living

[7] Plants—Making Food

Warm Up

Collect a leaf and paste it here.

Write its shape _____

Write the colour _____

Write the texture _____

The kind of edge it has _____

When you feel hungry, you eat food. Animals too eat food when they feel hungry. All living beings need food to live. Plants also need food to live, but unlike animals, they do not eat food. Instead, they make their own food.

A plant prepares its food in its green leaves.

Parts of a Leaf

Leaf blade

The flat broad surface of the leaf is called the **leaf blade**. It helps to trap the maximum amount of sunlight.

Veins

The main vein runs along the centre of the leaf. It is called the **midrib**. It has a number of side veins. The veins are small tubes that supply water brought by the stem and branches to all parts of the leaf. They also take the food prepared by the leaf to the stem, which supplies the food to the other parts of the plant.

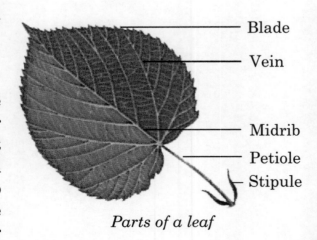

— Blade

— Vein

— Midrib

— Petiole

— Stipule

Parts of a leaf

50

Stomata

The leaf has minute pores or openings called **stomata**. There are more stomata on the lower surface of the leaf. Air enters and leaves the leaf through these stomata. Water vapour too is released through the stomata.

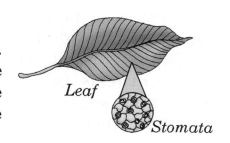
Leaf
Stomata

Petiole

The petiole or the stalk of the leaf attaches the leaf blade to the stem. It helps in the supply of water and food similar to the stem.

Stipule

Stipules are small leaf-like pair that are found at the base of the petiole of many flowering plants.

Now you know

Fill in the blanks.

- The flat broad surface of the leaf is called the _____.
- The main vein of the leaf is called the _____.
- The minute pores on the leaf are called the _____.

Making of Food in the Leaves

The leaf is like the kitchen of the plant.

Leaves have a green substance called **chlorophyll**. The chlorophyll absorbs sunlight that falls on the leaf. At the same time, carbon dioxide from the air enters the leaf through the stomata. Water absorbed by the roots moves upwards and reaches the leaf through the stem and the veins.

Chlorophyll uses sunlight for energy and changes water and carbon dioxide gas into **sugar**. This sugar is the plant's food.

Do you know?

- Cactus plants do not have leaves. They have stems which are green in colour. So their stems prepare the food.
- Mushrooms are not green and cannot make their own food. These plants live on dead matter.

Cactus   *Mushrooms*

This process of preparing food from carbon dioxide and water by using sunlight is called **photosynthesis** (*photo* means 'light' and *synthesis* means 'putting together').

During photosynthesis, oxygen is produced by the leaf and is given out through the stomata.

The food prepared by photosynthesis is used for the growth of the plant. Extra food is changed into a substance called **starch** and stored in different parts of the plant.

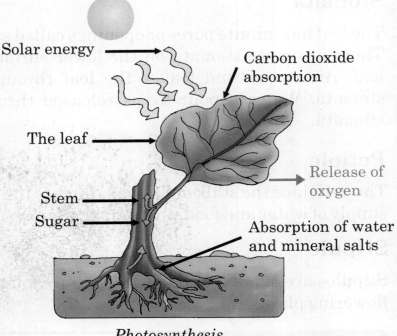

Solar energy

Carbon dioxide absorption

The leaf

Release of oxygen

Stem

Sugar

Absorption of water and mineral salts

Photosynthesis

52

To show that stored food in potato is starch.

Take a bottle of dilute iodine solution. It is pale yellow or brown in colour. But when iodine comes in contact with starch, its colour changes to blue-black.

Take a slice of potato and add a few drops of dilute iodine solution to its cut surface.

Observe the change. The iodine solution changes to blue-black. This shows that potato contains starch.

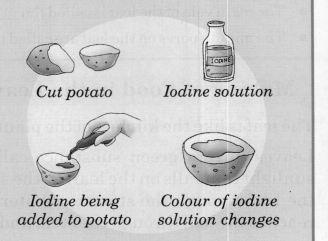

Cut potato

Iodine solution

Iodine being added to potato

Colour of iodine solution changes

Now you know

Fill in the blanks.

- The _____ is like the kitchen of the plant.
- The _____ in leaves uses sunlight for energy.
- The food prepared by the leaf is in the form of _____.

Energy Flow in Living Things

We have just seen that plants trap the energy of sunlight to prepare food. They use some of this energy for their growth. But some energy is stored in their body in the form of starch.

The energy in starch is transferred to animals when they eat plant food. Animals use part of this energy to work and grow, and store a part of the energy in their body.

When some other animals eat these animals, the energy again passes into the body of the meat-eater in the form of food.

This forms a kind of chain where energy flows from the sun to the plants and then to animals in the form of food. Such chain is called a **food chain**.

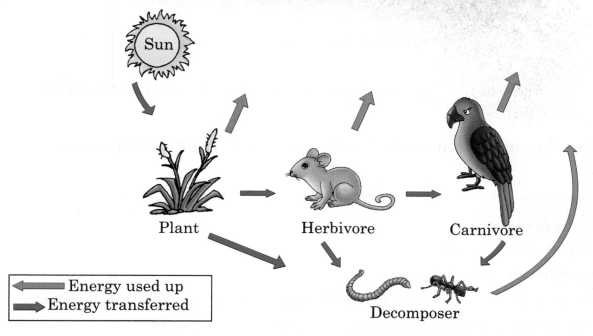

Energy flow in a food chain

Animals and Plants Depend on Each Other

Green plants give human beings and animals food in the form of vegetables, fruits, nuts and grains. Animals cannot live without this food.

Plants also release oxygen during photosynthesis and freshen up the air. Oxygen is used for breathing by animals and human beings.

In turn, animals breathe out carbon dioxide which the plants need to prepare food.

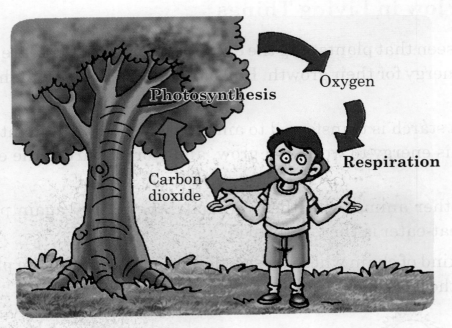

Photosynthesis

Oxygen

Respiration

Carbon dioxide

Gas exchange between plants and animals

54   When animals die, their dead remains mix in the soil and form important nutrients for the plants.

So you can see that plants and animals depend on each other in many ways.

Points to Remember

- Plants prepare their own food.
- The leaf prepares food for the plant.
- The different parts of a leaf are the leaf blade, the veins, the stomata and the petiole.
- The process by which the leaf prepares food is called photosynthesis.
- Energy flows from the sun to the plants and then to animals.
- Plants and animals depend on each other.

 New Words

Leaf blade: the flat broad surface of the leaf

Stomata: the minute pores or openings on the leaf

Chlorophyll: the green substance in the leaf

Photosynthesis: the process by which the leaf prepares food

Exercises

A. Fill in the blanks with the correct option.

1. The _____ traps maximum sunlight.   midrib/leaf blade

2. Air enters and leaves the leaf through the _____.
   stomata/veins

3. Plants produce _____ during photosynthesis.
   sugar/carbon dioxide

4. In cactus, photosynthesis takes place in the _____.
   roots/stem

B. Name the following.

1. The flat broad surface of the leaf.   _____

2. The vein which runs along the centre of the leaf.   _____

3. The minute pores on a leaf.   _____

4. The green substance in the leaf.   _____

5. The process through which a leaf prepares food.   _____

6. A plant in which the food is prepared by the stem.   _____

C. Answer these questions.

1. Draw and label a diagram of the parts of a leaf.

2. What is the function of the veins in a leaf?

3. Write a short note on the role of stomata in the leaf.

4. What does a plant require to make food?

5. Does photosynthesis take place twenty-four hours of the day? Why?

6. What food does the plant prepare?

7. With a neat, labelled diagram show how plants and animals depend on each
   other for the gases they need.

Fill in the crossword by using the clues given.

Across:

1. Gas used by plants for making food
2. Extra food stored in plants
3. Process of making food in plants

Down:

1. Green pigment present in leaf
2. Gas released by plants during photosynthesis
3. Pores in the leaf
4. Chemical used to test the presence of starch

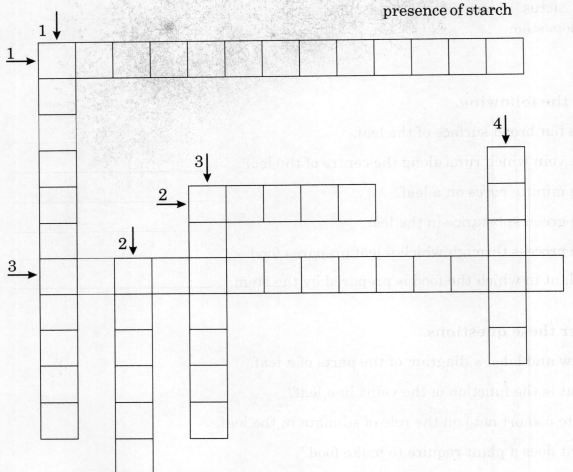

Brainstorm

1. What will happen if a green plant is kept in a closed, dark room for a long time?
2. Find out and write what green plants give us.

Project Idea

Draw a diagram of photosynthesis and make banners on 'Grow More Trees' and 'Save Trees'.

Unit 3: The World of the Living

[8] Adaptations in Plants

Warm Up

Tick (✓) mark the correct option for each of the following.

1. A plant that grows in water.

2. A plant that grows in deserts.

3. A plant that grows in mountains.

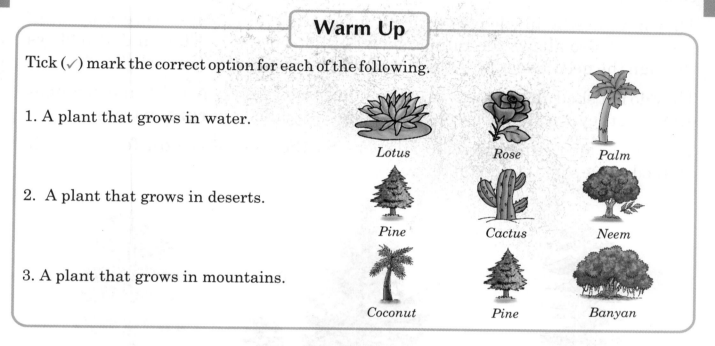

Lotus   Rose   Palm

Pine   Cactus   Neem

Coconut   Pine   Banyan

Plants grow almost everywhere in the world. They grow both in land and water. Plants which live on land are called **terrestrial** plants and plants that live in water are called **aquatic** plants.

Terrestrial plants

Aquatic plants

Plants need soil, water, warmth and sunlight to grow. But all the places do not have the same kind of soil or the same amount of water, warmth or sunlight. Plants adjust to their surroundings by making a few changes in themselves. The natural process by which plants adjust to their surroundings is called **adaptation.**

Let us see how terrestrial and aquatic plants adapt to the various conditions in which they grow.

Adaptations in Terrestrial Plants

Plants in mountains

In mountains and hilly areas, it is very cold in winters. Many areas experience snowfall and heavy winds. It also rains very often in hilly areas. The trees are tall and straight. The branches often slope downwards for the snow to fall off easily.

They have needle-like leaves with a waxy coating. This helps to prevent loss of water and also allows the rain or snow to slide off easily. The wind also blows through the needles easily without making the trees sway too much.

They do not shed all their leaves at the same time. A few leaves fall and new ones grow. So, they are always green. These trees are called **evergreen** trees.

These trees bear **cones** instead of flowers. So, they are called **conifers**. Pine, fir and cedar are some of the conifers.

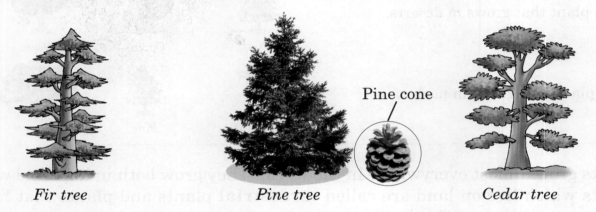

Fir tree   *Pine tree*   Pine cone   *Cedar tree*

Plants in plains

In the plains, the trees which grow in hot areas have lots of branches and leaves. Most of the trees shed all their leaves at the same time once in a year. These trees are called **deciduous** trees. Peepal, banyan, neem and gulmohar are some such trees.

Peepal tree   *Banyan tree*   *Neem tree*   *Gulmohar tree*

In places which are hot and damp with a lot of rainfall, the trees are evergreen. Rubber, teak, tamarind, pepper and coconut are some of the plants that grow in such places.

Rubber trees

Teak trees

Coconut trees

Plants in deserts

In deserts, it is very hot and there is very little rain. Even then, some plants grow there. Most desert plants grow roots that spread out just below the surface of the ground so that the roots can absorb most of the water that falls on the ground. Some grow roots that go deep down into the soil in search of water.

Cactus   *Date palm*

Most desert plants have very few leaves with a waxy coating. In many other plants, the leaves are modified into **spines**. The spines prevent loss of water and also protect the plant from animals.

The stems are green and help in photosynthesis. The stems are also fleshy because they store water. The waxy coating on the stems and leaves prevents loss of water.

Plants in marshy areas

In marshy lands, the soil is clayey and covered with water. The roots of the trees that grow here do not get air from the soil. So, they grow out of the soil and water to breathe. These roots are called **breathing roots**. The roots also hold the tree above water like stilts. These plants are called **mangroves**.

Mangroves

Now you know

Fill in the blanks.

- Pine trees have needle-like _____.
- Banyan is a _____ type of tree.
- Rubber and coconut grow in _____ and _____ places.
- Spines in a cactus plant prevent loss of _____.
- Trees which grow in marshy lands are known as _____.

Adaptations in Aquatic Plants

Aquatic plants are of three types—floating plants, fixed plants and underwater plants.

Floating plants

Some plants like water hyacinth and duckweed float on water. These plants are spongy and filled with air. This makes the plants very light and helps them to float on water.

Water hyacinth

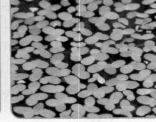
Duckweed

Fixed plants

Some plants like lotus and water lily have roots that fix the plant in the mud at the bottom of the pond. Their stems are hollow and have air spaces.

Lotus

Water lily

This helps the flowers and leaves to float on water. The broad and flat leaves spread over the surface of water to catch maximum sunlight. The leaves have stomata only on the upper side of the leaf. The leaves have a waxy coating to repel water.

60

Underwater plants

Some plants like hydrilla and tape grass grow under water. They are completely submerged in water. The leaves and stems are thin and flexible. This allows them to move with water currents. They have narrow, thin leaves with no stomata. They breathe through their body surface.

Hydrilla

Tape grass

Now you know

Fill in the blanks.

• Water _____ plant floats on water.

• The roots of water _____ are fixed in the mud at the bottom of the pond.

• The _____ grass plant is completely submerged in water.

Some Unusual Plants

Non-green plants

Some plants do not make their own food. Plants like mushroom and toadstool do not have chlorophyll and so cannot make their own food by photosynthesis. They absorb food from dead remains of living things like wood and litter.

Mushroom

Toadstool

Epiphytes

Some plants like mosses, ferns and many orchids grow on other plants. This allows them to reach positions where they can have better access to sunlight. These plants are known as **epiphytes**.

Moss

Orchid

As their roots are not in the soil, they absorb moisture from the air. Their leaves are capable of absorbing nutrients from plant parts which fall on them.

Insectivorous plants

Some plants like venus flytrap and pitcher plant catch insects in special traps made from their modified leaves.

Venus flytrap

Pitcher plant

Grasses

Grass does not need as much water as the trees or bushes. It grows in wide open spaces. When the grass does not get water, it dries up. But the seeds and stems remain alive in the soil. As soon as it rains, it grows again.

Unlike other plants, the leaves of grass do not grow at the tips. They grow from the base so that even when animals graze on them, the grass grows quickly again.

The rainforest

There is a lot of rainfall in the rainforests. The rainforests are hot and damp. That is why many trees grow here. The evergreen trees often grow very tall. They grow so close to each other that it is difficult for sunlight to reach the ground. There are many climbers which twine around the trees and climb up towards sunlight. The flowers which grow here are colourful.

62

Do you know?

Trees in the rainforests are being cut down for wood or to clear the land for their use by many people. It is also affecting the animals living in these areas. So, both the forests and the animals are in danger of extinction and once lost, they cannot be replaced.

Points to Remember

- The natural process by which plants adjust to their surroundings is called adaptation.
- Plants which grow on land are called terrestrial plants.
- Some trees which are always green are called evergreen trees.
- Some trees which shed all their leaves once a year are called deciduous trees.
- In hilly areas, plants have needle-like leaves. In the plains, plants have lots of branches and leaves. In the desert, plants have no leaves.
- In marshy areas, plants have breathing roots.
- Aquatic plants float or are submerged in water.
- Non-green plants like mushroom and toadstool absorb food from dead remains of living things.
- Epiphytes grow on other plants.
- There is a lot of rainfall in the rainforest.

New Words

Terrestrial plants: plants which grow on land

Aquatic plants: plants that grow in water

Evergreen: a plant which has green leaves throughout the year

Deciduous: trees that shed their leaves at the same time once in a year

Waxy: looking like wax

Marshy: ground near a lake, river or sea, that is always wet

Epiphyte: a plant that grows on another plant but does not depend on it for its own nutrients

Insectivorous: able to catch and digest insects

Exercises

A. Fill in the blanks with the correct option.

1. Plants which grow on land are called _____ plants.   aquatic/terrestrial

2. Plants which do not shed all their leaves at the same time are called _____. deciduous/evergreen

3. Plants which grow in marshy lands are called _____.
   mangroves/conifers

4. The leaves of fixed aquatic plants have stomata on the _____ side of the leaf. upper/lower

5. Underwater plants have narrow thin leaves with no _____.
   stomata/leaves

6. Flat, broad leaves of a plant get _____ sunlight.
   minimum/maximum

B. Match the following.

1. cedar   a. desert

2. peepal   b. under water

3. pepper   c. marshy lands

4. cactus   d. hilly area

5. mangroves   e. hot and damp place

6. tape grass   f. plains

63

C. Complete these sentence.

1. Deciduous trees shed _____

2. Breathing roots are found in trees that _____

3. Floating plants are spongy and _____

4. Grass grows from the _____

5. Rainforests are hot _____

D. Answer these questions.

1. What is adaptation?
2. Which trees are called evergreen trees?
3. What are the adaptations of the trees in hilly areas?
4. Name the three types of aquatic plants.
5. What helps the floating plants to float on water?
6. Describe the adaptations in a lotus plant.
7. Why is a rainforest so called?

Task

Draw a cactus plant and answer the following.

1. Why do the roots of a cactus plant spread out just below the surface of the ground?

_____

2. Why do they grow spines instead of leaves?

_____

3. Why are the stems fleshy?

_____

4. Which part of the plant prepares food?

_____

Brainstorm

Collect information on some unusual plants and write how they adapt themselves to their surroundings.

Project Idea

From your school library, get some information on the plants and animals found in a rainforest. Draw or paste their pictures and write information about them. You can make a file. Decorate and make your project look attractive.

Unit 3: The World of the Living

[9] Adaptations in Animals

Can you see the animals hiding in the pictures? Name them by unscrambling the letters.

ONIL: _____

GERTI: _____

LOW: _____

XOF: _____

Animals are found all over the world. Some animals live in hot places and some live in cold places. Some live in high mountains, some in deep oceans. The natural surroundings where an animal lives is called its **habitat**.

As the living conditions in different habitats are different, the animals living in a particular habitat have to adapt themselves to live in their habitat.

For animals, adaptation means having certain body parts or behaviours that help them to survive and thrive in their surroundings. It takes many years for animals to adapt themselves to their surroundings.

Adaptations to Habitat

Depending upon whether an animal lives on land, water or air, it possesses various features which enable it to survive in its own habitat.

Terrestrial animals

Animals that live on land are called **terrestrial animals**. Lions, tigers, horses, dogs and cats are some of the terrestrial animals. Their body is suited to live on land. Accordingly, they show different adaptive features.

Land animals breathe air directly from the atmosphere. So, most of them have **lungs**. Insects do not have lungs. They breathe with the help of air holes called **spiracles** present on their body surface.

Land animals have well-developed **sense organs** which keep them aware of the presence of food or dangers around them.

Animals in plains: Most animals which live on hard land surface like forests and grasslands have strong legs to run fast. This helps them to catch their prey or run away from their enemies.

Grass-eating animals like horses and cows have toes in the form of **hoofs** which help them move on soft and wet land.

Lion

Tiger

Horse

Cow

Burrowing animals like rabbits and moles have sharp claws to dig the ground and make burrows.

Rabbit

Mole

Snake

Snakes live in narrow **holes** in anthills, trees or holes made by other animals. So they do not have legs. They move by pushing against the ground with their tough scales.

Mountain goat and yak

Animals in mountains: Animals like mountain goats and yaks living in the cold conditions of high mountains have a thick coat of hair to protect themselves against the severe cold.

Mountain goats are surefooted. They can run up vertical rocks and can sit on very narrow ledges.

Animals in deserts: The camel is the best example of desert adaptation. It has broad, padded feet to walk comfortably on sand. After the camel eats food, the extra food and water changes to fat and gets stored in the camel's hump. Then the camel can go on for days without food and water. Camels have long, thick eyelashes to keep them safe from sand during sandstorms. They are also able to close their nose during a sandstorm.

To beat the daytime heat, many desert animals such as desert rats come out in search of food only during the night time. Some animals stay inside their holes during the hot summer months without eating any food. This long period of summer sleep is known as **aestivation**.

Camel

Animals in cold and snow bound regions: The snow leopard which lives in the snowy mountains of the Himalayas has a thick white coat of hair on its body. The polar bear and the polar fox living in the ice bound arctic polar region have thick white fur on their body. The fur not only protects them from the severe cold, but the white colour also makes them less visible against the white background. This helps them to approach their food without being noticed.

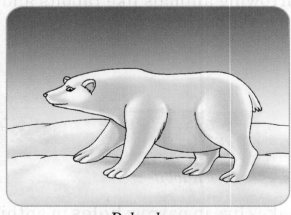
Polar bear

Animals like seals, walruses and penguins have a thick layer of fat called **blubber** which keeps their body warm in the cold freezing conditions.

Most birds survive the winter by going to warmer places. This is called **migration**. They return to their original homes when the winter is over.

Seal

Walrus

Penguins

Most birds survive the winter by going to warmer places. This is called **migration**. They return to their original homes when the winter is over.

Migratory birds

Snake

Frogs, snakes, lizards and many insects survive the winter by going into a long period of rest. They don't eat or drink during this period. They keep lying in a safe place like a cave, hole or burrow to save energy. This period of winter sleep is called **hibernation**.

Arboreal animals

Animals which spend a lot of time on trees are called **arboreal animals**. Their body is suited to live in trees.

They have long and strong limbs with sharp claws to climb the trees. The monkey and the chameleon have long tails to grip the branches. The tails also help the arboreal animals to balance their body.

Chameleon

Monkey

Aerial animals

Animals that can fly in the air are called **aerial animals**. Birds and bats fly in the air. Birds have wings to fly with. They also have hollow bones which make their body light and help them fly.

Bats are not birds. They are mammals. They do not have true wings. Their wings are made of flaps of skin.

Many insects also have wings which help them fly in the air.

Bat

Birds

Aquatic animals

Animals that live in water are called **aquatic animals**. Fish, crabs, seals and seahorses are some of the animals that live in water.

Fish have fins to swim with. Turtles, seals and dolphins have oar-like flippers to swim in water.

Aquatic animals

Animals like fish, prawn and crab which live inside water have **gills** to breathe oxygen dissolved in water. Some aquatic animals like whales and dolphins breathe through lungs. So, they come to the surface of water very often to breathe air. Water birds like ducks and swans have webbed feet which help them to paddle in water.

Amphibians

Animals which live both on land and in water are called **amphibians**. Frogs, toads and salamander are some of the amphibians. Baby frogs are known as tadpoles. They grow in water and have gills for breathing. Adult frogs have lungs to breathe on land. They also breathe through their skin when in water. Frogs have webbed hind feet to swim in water.

Frog

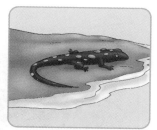
Salamander

Now you know

Fill in the blanks.

- Mountain goats are _____ footed.
- Snakes move by pushing against the ground with their _____.
- Turtles have _____ to swim in the water.

Adaptations for Food

Animals eat plants or other animals. Parts of their body are adapted to find food and eat it. The shape of their teeth depends on the food they eat.

Herbivores

Plant-eating animals like cows, goats, deer, giraffe and elephants are known as herbivores. They have sharp front teeth to cut the grass and flat grinding teeth to grind leaves, seeds and twigs. Giraffes have long necks to reach the leaves of tall trees. Elephants have a trunk.

Rabbit

Carnivores

Flesh-eating animals like lions, tigers and foxes are known as carnivores. They have sharp, pointed teeth to tear the flesh and strong jaws to grip their prey. Their strong legs and claws help them to run fast and catch their prey.

Fox

Carnivorous birds like eagles, hawks and owls have keen eyesight to spot their prey from the sky. They have strong claws to hold their prey and sharp, hooked beaks to tear the flesh.

Owl

Giant anteaters feed on termites as well as ants with the help of tongues which are up to half a metre long. Their long hair and thick skin protects them from the bites of angry ants and termites defending their nest.

Parasites

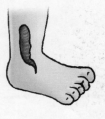

Parasites are small creatures which live on or inside the body of other animals or hosts. They depend on the hosts for their food.

Ticks, fleas and some mosquitoes suck blood from the hosts.

Leech

Tick

72

Worms like hookworms, tapeworms and roundworms live inside the body of animals and take their nutrition from the host body.

Sometimes birds have parasites on their bodies. To get rid of the parasites, they go and disturb an ant's nest. The ants run all over the bird's body and when they find the parasites sticking to the bird's body, they eat them.

Adapting to be Safe

Some animals like grasshoppers, toads, butterflies, leaf insects and stick insects hide from their enemies by having body colour or shape that blend with their surroundings.

Grasshopper   *Toad*   *Butterfly*   *Leaf insect*   *Stick insect*

Similarly, many hunting animals like tigers and lions also avoid being seen by their prey by having body colour or stripes and spots on their body that help them blend with the surroundings.

This kind of blending into the background is called **camouflage**.

Tiger

Lion

Porcupine

Some animals behave in a peculiar way to be safe from their enemies.

The porcupine puffs out the quills. The quills easily come loose if touched and stick to the enemy's skin. They can cause painful wounds or infection.

A pangolin's back is covered with overlapping scales. It tucks its head between its legs and rolls itself into a ball when it senses danger.

Pangolin

A pangolin rolls itself into a ball

73

Now you know

Give one example of each of the following.

- An animal which has a keen eyesight to spot the prey. _____
- A small creature which lives inside the body of another animal. _____
- An animal which camouflages itself in snow. _____

Points to Remember

- The natural surrounding of an animal is known as its habitat.
- Animals adapt to their habitats by developing special body features or behaviour.
- Terrestrial animals have lungs and well-developed sense organs.
- Animals living in the plains have strong legs to run.
- Grass-eating animals have hoofs to walk on soft land.
- Burrowing animals have sharp claws to dig soil or have no legs at all.
- Animals living in cold places have a coat of thick furs and blubbers to beat the cold.
- Many animals and birds living in cold places migrate to warmer places in winter.
- Some animals hibernate in the winter.
- Arboreal animals have long and strong limbs with sharp claws to climb the trees.
- Many animals have wings to fly in the air.
- Aquatic animals have fins to move and gills to breathe.
- Animals which live on water have webbed feet.
- Amphibians develop features of both terrestrial and aquatic animals.
- Herbivores have sharp front teeth and flat grinding teeth to eat plant parts.
- Carnivores have sharp pointed teeth, strong jaws, claws and legs.
- Parasitic animals depend on the hosts for their food.
- Many animals use camouflage to avoid recognition by their enemies or preys.

New Words

Habitat: natural surroundings where animals live

Thrive: to grow or develop without difficulty

Surefooted: to be able to walk easily, without falling

Ledge: a narrow shelf which sticks out from a vertical surface

Parasite: small creatures which live on or inside the body of other animals

Aestivation: the long inactive stage of an animal during the summer

Hibernation: long winter sleep of animals

Camouflage: the natural colouring of animals which enable them to blend with the surroundings

Exercises

A. Fill in the blanks with the correct option.

1. The natural surroundings where an animal lives is called its _____ .
   habit/habitat

2. Animals that live on land are called _____ animals.
   terrestrial/arboreal

3. Birds and _____ can fly in the air. rabbits/bats

4. _____ live on or inside the body of other animals.
   Herbivores/Parasites

5. The quills of a _____ can cause painful wounds. porcupine/pangolin

B. Match the following.

1. animals that live on land   a. aquatic
2. long winter sleep   b. aerial
3. animals that live both in land and water c. hibernation
4. animals that can fly   d. terrestrial
5. animals that live in water   e. amphibian

C. Answer these questions.

1. What is habitat?
2. What are the adaptive features of terrestrial animals?
3. What helps a monkey to climb trees?
4. What helps aquatic animals to move around in water?
5. What are the adaptations of animals hunting in water for food?
6. What is camouflage?
7. How does a pangolin keep itself safe from its enemies?

Task

Identify the animals with the following adaptive features.

1. I am a hunter with strong legs and stripes on my body.   _____

2. I have broad feet to walk on sand.   _____

3. I live in a hole and have no legs.   _____

4. My wings are made of flaps of skin.   _____

5. I can live both in land and water. _____

6. I bite and suck your blood. _____

Brainstorm

Find information about behavioural adaptations of two animals. Draw or paste their pictures and write the information.

Project Idea

1. Make a chart of animals that adapt themselves by blending in the surroundings.
2. Make a chart on the adaptive features of a camel.

76

Unit 4: Moving Things, People and Ideas

[10] Force, Work and Energy

Warm Up

What makes these toys move?
Choose the correct word and write it below each picture.

Push, Pull, Winding, Battery

winding   battery   pull   push

Force

You already know that pushes and pulls are forces. When you push or pull something, it moves. When you throw a ball, you use force. When you hit a moving ball, you use force to change its direction. When you stop a moving ball, you use force.

Using force to move: bowl a cricket ball

Using force to change direction: hit a cricket ball

Using force to stop: catch a cricket ball

77

Therefore, force can

- move a body
- change the direction of a moving body, and
- stop a moving body.

Force can also change the shape of a body.

Force can change the shape of an object

Types of force

When you use your muscles to move things, you use **muscular force**. Animals use muscular force when they use their muscles to pull a load.

Using muscular force

When you throw a ball up in the air, it comes down. This is because the earth pulls everything towards itself. This pull or force which pulls all the things towards the centre of the earth is called **gravitational force**.

Gravitational force

A moving body stops due to **frictional force**. When we roll a ball along the ground, it stops after some time. As its surface grazes along the rough surface of the ground, the resulting force stops the ball. This force is known as **frictional force**.

Frictional force

Now you know

Fill in the blanks.

- When muscles are used to move a thing, ___muscular___ force is used.
- ___gravitational___ force pulls things towards the centre of the earth.
- A moving body stops due to ___frictional___ force.

78

Work

Work is done when an object is moved through a distance by using force. When we push or pull a body, work is done only when the body moves. In science, work is not done if a body is not moved from its original position, even if force is applied. For example, when you push a wall, you apply force. But the wall does not move. So, no work is done. But when you kick a ball, the ball moves from its original position. So work is done.

Child pushing a wall

Child kicking a ball

Simple Machines

Sometimes we find it hard to do certain work with our hand. So we use simple tools, such as a screwdriver to fix a screw, a hammer to drive a nail or a knife to cut vegetables. These tools make our work easy. These are called **machines**. These tools are very simple, and do not have too many parts or attachments. So these are called **simple machines.** There are six types of simple machines.

Types of simple machines

1. **A lever** is used to lift or move things. Pliers, tongs and nut crackers are some examples of levers.

Lever

2. **A pulley** is made from a wheel and rope. It is used to raise, lower or move a load. It is used to draw water from the wells, to hoist a flag, or to lift a weight in a crane, etc.

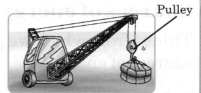

Pulley

Pulley

3. **Wheel and axle** is made up of two circular objects in which one object is bigger than the other. One is a wheel and the other is an axle. Giant wheel and bicycle pedal are some of the examples of wheel and axle.

Wheel and axle

4. An **inclined plane** is a slope. It makes it easier to lift something heavy. Instead of lifting something heavy straight up, you can push it up an inclined plane with less force.

Inclined plane

5. **Wedge** has sharp edges on one side and blunt on the other. It is used to cut or split objects. Knife and axe are examples of wedges.

Wedge

6. **Screw** is a thin cone with a spiral ridge or thread running round it.

Screw

Now you know

Fill in the blanks.

- A _lever_ is used to lift or move things.
- _axle_ is a thin cone with a spiral ridge.
- The different types of simple machines are _lever_, _pulley_, _wedge_, _screw_, _wheel and axle_ and _plane_.

Do you know?

Machines like cars, cranes and computers are complex machines. Complex machines are a combination of two or more simple machines.

80

Energy

Energy is the capacity to do work. We need energy to do various kinds of work.

Sources of energy

Things from which we get energy are called sources of energy. There are different sources of energy.

Solar energy: Sun is the main source of energy. The energy that we get from the sun is called solar energy.

We get heat and light from the sun. The green plants trap this energy and make food. Plants, animals and human beings use this food to get energy.

We get fuels such as wood and coal from the plants. They have stored heat energy in them.

Thus, the energy that we get from plants is stored solar energy.

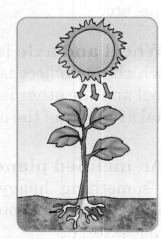
Plants trap solar energy

Solar energy is also used in solar cookers and solar heaters, etc.

Solar heater

Solar cooker

Wind energy: When wind blows, it moves the blades of a windmill and produces electricity. Thus, wind is a source of energy.

Wind mills use the energy of the wind

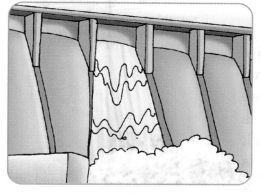
Energy of flowing water is used to produce electricity

Water energy: Water can turn a wheel. Dams are built to check water from flowing down a river. Dams have gates. The gates are opened to release the water with great force. The water gushes down and turns the wheels called turbines to produce electricity. Thus, water is a source of energy.

Geothermal energy: The heat stored inside the earth is also a source of energy. This is called geothermal energy. It is used to produce electricity.

Heat energy inside the earth is used to produce electricity

Do you know?

Sources of energy like wood, coal and petrol have been in use for many years. They are in limited supply and may get used up completely one day. They also cause pollution. So, they have to be used with care.

Forms of energy

Energy is found in different forms, such as light, heat, sound and motion. There are many forms of energy.

You must have seen the working of fans and mixers in your house. These machines work on electricity. So, **electricity is a form of energy**. Some trains too run on electricity but some trains burn fuel like coal and diesel and work on the heat produced. So, **heat too is a form of energy**.

A fan works on electricity

If you hold a magnifying glass in the hot sun and try to concentrate the light rays at one point on a piece of paper, after some time, the paper starts burning. It shows that **light is a form of energy**.

You can break off a fruit high up on a tree by throwing a stone. The moving objects have energy called **mechanical energy**.

A train runs on fuel

We use electricity to play music systems or radio. Here, electrical energy gets converted to **sound energy**. Like this, we can burn lights in our house with the help of electricity. Here electrical energy is converted into light energy. Many machines work on electricity. In these cases, electrical energy is converted into mechanical energy. Energy can be changed from one form to another.

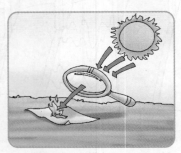
Light can burn things

Points to Remember

- Force can move a body, change the direction of a moving body, stop a moving body and change the shape of a body.

- There are different types of forces.

- Work is done only when an object is moved through a distance using force.

- Simple machines make work easier for us.

- Lever, pulley, wheel and axle, inclined plane, wedge and screw are the different types of simple machines.

- Energy is the capacity to do work.

- Things from which we get energy are called sources of energy.

- Energy is found in different forms, such as light, heat, sound and motion.

- Energy can be changed from one form to another.

Simple machines: tools which do not have too many parts or attachments
Energy: capacity to do work
Solar energy: energy from the sun
Geothermal energy: energy from the hot interior of the earth

Exercises

A. Fill in the blanks with the correct option.

1. When you use your muscles to move things, you use ___*Mus*___ force.
   mechanical/muscular

2. ___*Work*___ is done when an object moves. Energy/Work

3. A tool which does not have many parts is called a ___*simp*___ machine.
   simple/complicated

4. Plants prepare food with the help of _____ energy. solar/mechanical

5. The _____ is a source of energy. sun/moon

B. Tick the situations where work is done in the park.

1. A boy kicks a ball and the ball moves far away.

2. His friend runs after the ball and kicks it gently and the ball moves just a short distance.

3. A child tries unsuccessfully to lift his mother's heavy bag.

4. Another child is swinging on a swing.

5. A child is sliding down on a slide.

C. Answer these questions.

1. Define force.

2. Name any two types of forces.

3. Draw and name any two simple machines.

4. When is work said to be done?

5. Write a short note on solar energy.

6. Name two devices which use solar energy.

7. Which type of energy is used to fly a kite?

83

Task

Look at this picture of a construction site. Name the simple machines which you can see being used.

Brainstorm

Give five examples of electrical energy changing to mechanical energy.

Project Idea

Visit a railway station and observe the different simple machines used there.

Unit 5: Natural Phenomena

[11] Air, Water and Weather

Warm Up

Complete the sentences.

- On a hot sunny day, I _____

- On a cold day, I _____

- On a rainy day, I _____

Air

Air is a mixture of gases. Our earth is surrounded by a layer of air called **atmosphere**. Moving air is called **wind**.

A light wind is called a **breeze.** It causes leaves to rustle, small flags to flap, or even at times causes bushes and small trees to sway.

A very strong wind is called a **gale**. It makes walking difficult. Whole trees sway; branches break and tiles from roofs of houses are blown away.

A very strong wind which can uproot trees and cause damage to buildings is called a **storm**. When a storm is accompanied by thunder and rain, it is called a **thunderstorm**.

A wind blowing

Do you know?

The air is thicker near the ground and becomes thinner as we go up. Finally, where the layer of air ends, outer space begins.

What causes the winds to blow?

The heat of the sun heats up the air. Warm air is lighter than cold air, so it rises up and the cool air which is at the ground level, rushes in and takes its place. This sets off an air current, causing wind.

Sea breeze and land breeze

During the day, the land gets warmer faster than the water. The air above the land too becomes warm and rises up. The cool air from the sea moves in towards the land and takes its place. This is called **sea breeze**.

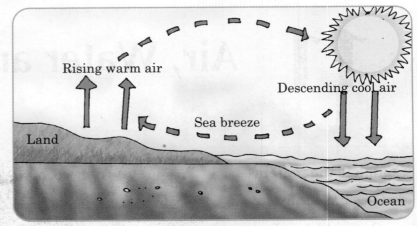

Sea breeze

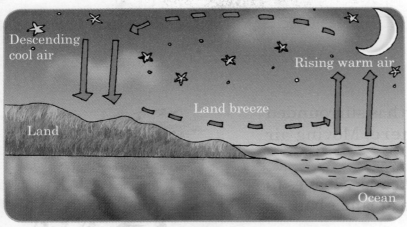

Land breeze

During the night, the land gets cooler faster than water. The air above the sea becomes warm and rises up. The cool air from the land moves in towards the sea and takes its place. This is called **land breeze**.

Activity

Take two plastic bowls. Fill one bowl with water and the other with sand. Keep both the bowls outside in the hot sun for one hour. Feel the hotness of the water and sand by touching. Which one is hotter?

Bring both these bowls inside the house and keep them under shade for another one hour. Feel the temperature of the sand and water again. Which one is warmer?

What does this tell you?

Bowls in the sun

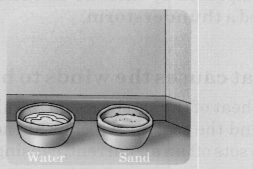

Bowls inside the room

Condensation

The process of water vapour changing to liquid water is called **condensation**.

Activity

Boil some water in a kettle. You will see steam or water vapour rising from the spout of the kettle. Ask an adult to hold a cold metal plate over the steam. You will see drops of water on the plate. The steam has changed to drops of water on cooling. After the water from the kettle cools down, check the amount of water left in the kettle. Note down your observation.

Steam

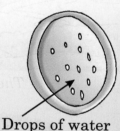
Drops of water

Water turns to steam on boiling

Steam turns to water on cooling

89

Freezing

When liquid water is cooled to zero degree Celsius (0 °C), it changes to a solid form known as ice. This process of changing water from liquid form to solid form is called **freezing**.

Ice

Activity

Fill an ice tray with water and keep it in the freezer of your refrigerator. After a few hours, remove the ice tray. You will notice that the liquid water in the ice tray has frozen and changed to solid form, which is ice.

The Water Cycle

Evaporation and condensation take place in nature too. Water on the surface of rivers, lakes, ponds and oceans gets heated up by the heat of the sun and evaporates. It rises up in the air. As the water vapour reaches the upper parts of the atmosphere, it cools down and condenses as tiny droplets of water to form clouds. The water droplets in the cloud further condense to form bigger drops of water which come down to the earth as rain. The rain water ultimately flows down to fill the different water bodies. This cycle of evaporation, condensation and subsequent return of water to the surface of earth is called the **water cycle**.

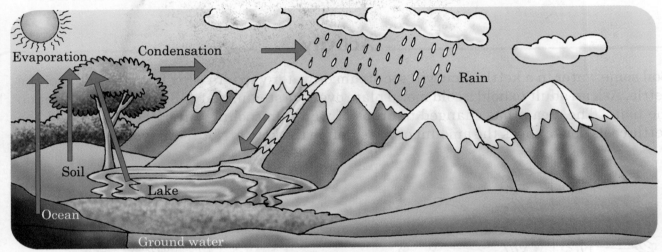

The water cycle

Do you know?

Rainbow is caused by sunlight falling on raindrops. When sunlight enters a raindrop, it gets separated into seven colours. To see a rainbow, you must stand with your back towards the sun and the rainfall in front of you.

In nature, evaporation and condensation of water cause rain, hail, dew, frost, fog and snow.

When it is cold, the raindrops freeze and turn into ice. This is called **hail**.

In winters, when water vapour condenses on cold objects like leaves, flowers and windowpanes, **dew** is formed.

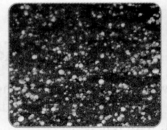

Hail

Dew

When it is extremely cold, the dew freezes into tiny white crystals called **frost**.

In winter, the water vapour in the air condenses on dust particles and forms a cloud just above the ground. This is called **fog**.

When water vapour cools suddenly, it freezes into tiny **snowflakes**.

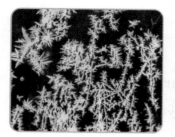
Frost

Fog

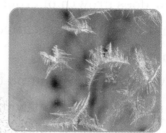
Snowflakes

Points to Remember

- Air is a mixture of gases.
- The sea breeze blows from the sea towards the land during the day.
- The land breeze blows from the land towards the sea at night.
- Weather is the state of the atmosphere at a place and time in relation to heat, cloudiness, dryness, sunshine, wind and rain.
- Sun causes changes in weather.
- Weather should be suitable for the proper growth of crops.
- Factors affecting rate of evaporation are temperature, wind and surface area.
- Evaporation and condensation of water make water cycle possible.
- Evaporation and condensation take place in nature too and cause rain, hail, dew, frost, fog and snow.

Exercises

A. Fill in the blanks with the correct option.

1. Our earth is surrounded by a layer of air called _____.
   atmosphere/storm

2. Warm air is _____ than cold air. heavier/lighter

3. The process in which water changes from liquid form to solid form is called _____. evaporation/freezing

4. When liquid water is cooled to 0 °C, it changes to _____. ice/steam

5. When it is cold, the raindrops freeze and turn into _____. hail/fog

B. Answer these questions.

1. With a neat diagram, write a note on sea breeze.
2. Define weather.
3. How does growth of crops depend on weather?
4. What are the factors affecting evaporation?
5. What is hail?
6. How do evaporation and condensation take place in nature?
7. Name the forms that water vapour takes on cooling.
8. What is the difference between dew and frost?

C. Correct the following sentences.

1. Water causes changes in weather.
2. During the night, water gets cooler faster than land.
3. The process in which water changes from liquid form to gaseous form is called condensation.
4. Clothes dry faster in winter than in summer.
5. Snow is frozen dewdrops.

92

Task

Draw an object on each poster which depicts three different types of weather on three different days.

Brainstorm

Rohit and Mohit are discussing water cycle. Rohit says, 'We get rains because of evaporation'. Mohit says, 'We get rains because of condensation'.

Who is right? Or, are both of them right, or both wrong?

What would you tell them to help settle their disagreement?

Project Idea

Show the journey of a water drop in the water cycle by drawing a series of pictures.

Unit 6: Natural Resources

[12] Soil

Identify the things which are usually made of clay and colour them brown.

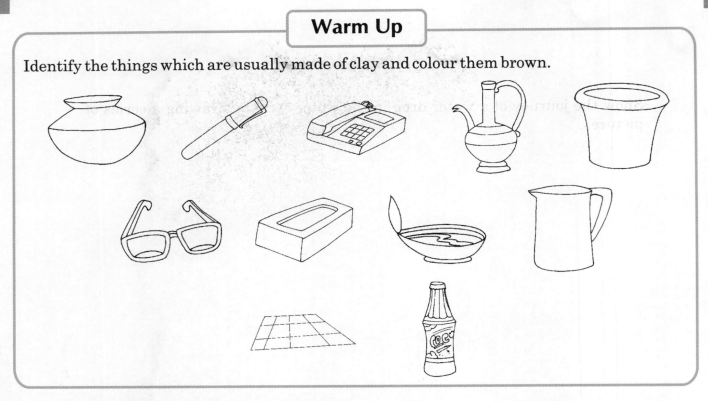

The outer soft layer of earth on which plants grow is known as **soil**. Soil is very important for life on earth. Plants need soil to grow on. Plants provide food to most animals. Plants also purify air and influence rainfall. So soil also indirectly plays an important role in supporting animal life, and influencing weather conditions. Without soil there will not be any plant life on land.

Plants need soil to grow on

How is Soil Formed?

Soil is formed by the breaking down of rocks into tiny particles. Rocks are hard and strong. But, they are constantly attacked by forces of nature such as **water** (rain and flowing water), **wind** and **heat**.

The constant action of winds, rains, flowing water and the heat of the sun weaken the binding power of the rocks. Rain water seeps into tiny cracks in the rocks. The cracks gradually open up. Over the years, tiny rock particles and dead remains of plants and animals get deposited in these cracks.

Some seeds sprout and plants grow in these cracks. As the plants grow bigger, the roots force the cracks wide open. Finally, pieces of rock split off and wear away. This process of wearing away of rocks is called **weathering of rocks**.

This process goes on for thousands of years till the large rocks break up into smaller particles and form soil.

1	2	3	4
Water and wind loosen up the rock surface and open up cracks	Remains of dead plants and animals get deposited in the cracks	Plant roots speed up weathering of rocks	Soil layer becomes deep enough for big trees to grow on it

What Does Soil Contain?

By now, you know that soil contains tiny bits of **rock particles**. Soil particles are of different sizes. The bigger particles of soil which are of the size of rice grains are called **gravel**. Smaller particles which are somewhat of the size of sugar grains are called **sand**. The very fine

Gravel

Sand

powder-like particles are called **clay**. Particles which are between the size of sand and clay are knows as **silt**.

Soil contains dead remains of plants and animals. It is known as **humus**.

Soil also contains **water** and **air**.

Silt   *Clay*

Activity

Aim: To see the different components of soil.

Materials needed: A water bottle, soil, water.

Humus
Water
Clay
Silt
Sand
Gravel

Method: Take an empty mineral water bottle through which you will be able to see the soil. Pour a cup of garden soil into it. Fill the bottle with water. Close its mouth with the cap and shake well. Let the bottle stand for about ten minutes. Now look at the water carefully. You will notice different layers of soil.

The gravel or the stones settle down at the bottom. Above that you will see the layer of sand. The silt layer settles above the sand. The clay settles on top of the silt. The top layer will have pieces of leaves, twigs, etc. This is the humus.

This experiment shows that soil contains particles of **gravel**, **sand**, **silt, clay** and **humus**.

Activity

Aim: To show that soil contains water.

Materials needed: A jar with lid, soil.

Method: Take some soil in a dry plastic jar. Cover it tightly with a lid. Keep it out in the hot sun. After half an hour remove the lid. You will see drops of water on the inside of the lid. This shows that soil contains **water**.

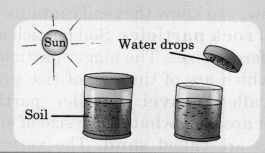

Sun   Water drops

Soil

Aim: To show that soil contains air.

Material: A jar, soil and water.

Method: Put some soil in a plastic jar. Pour water over it. You will see bubbles coming up. These are air bubbles. The air present in the soil comes up when water poured in the soil takes the place of air.

Now you know

Fill in the blanks.

- Rocks are constantly weathered by forces of nature such as _____, _____, and _____.

- Rocks wear away by the process of _____.

- Soil contains particles of _____, _____, _____, and _____.

Types of Soil

There are three main types of soil depending on the amount of the type of soil particles present in a soil.

Sandy soil

Sandy soil has more sand particles than gravel or clay. Its colour is usually brownish or grey. Sand grains are dry and hold air in the spaces between them. But this soil cannot hold water well. Sandy soil is usually found in deserts, river banks and at the seashore. Not many plants grow in this type of soil.

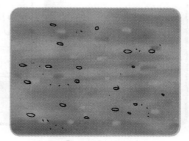

Sandy soil

Clayey soil

Clayey soil has a lot of clay particles. These stick together and can hold a lot of water. But there is no space for air in this soil. So, most plants cannot grow in this soil. Only a few plants like rice which need a lot of water grow in this soil. Potters use clayey soil to make pots.

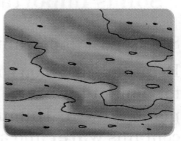

Clayey soil

97

Loam

Loam consists of a balanced quantity of sand, clay and humus. It can hold enough air and water for the plants to grow.

Loamy soil contains more nutrients and humus which makes the soil suitable for most plants to grow on it.

Loamy soil

Activity

Aim: To show that different types of soil allow different amounts of water to pass through them.

Materials needed: Three bottles, three funnels, three pieces of fine cloth, a glass, sand, clay, loam and water.

Method: Take three bottles. Keep a funnel on each bottle. Place a piece of fine cloth on each funnel. Push the cloth down the middle up to the neck of the funnel. Take care to see that the sides of the cloth remain outside the edge of the funnel. Put half a cup each of sand in the first funnel, clay in the second funnel and loam in the third funnel.

Pour a glass of water in each funnel.

Observe and note the amount of water that gets collected in each bottle.

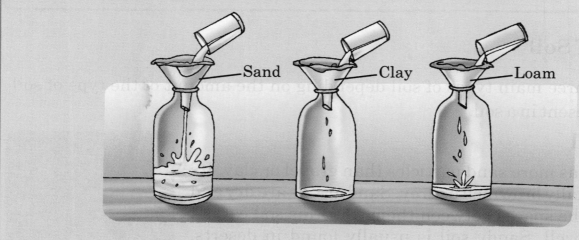

Soil is Important

Soil is most important to us because of its ability to let plants grow on it.

Plants can grow on soil because it contains all the necessary substances needed for a plant to survive. Soil particles contain **minerals** which are important for plant growth. Humus provides different **nutrients** to the plants. Soil also contains **water** and **air** needed by the plant.

Rocks contain different minerals in them. So, soil too has different colours. They can be black, red, brown or grey.

Black soil   Red soil   Brown soil   Grey soil

Different plants need different kind of soil.

Black soil is good for crops like cotton and sugar cane. Red soil is good for rice, wheat and sugar cane crops. Brown soil is good for tea, coffee, rubber and coconut.

Soil is also home to a variety of **animals**.

Earthworm   Ant   Centipede

99

Small animals like ants, bugs, centipedes and earthworms live in soil. Earthworms move through the soil creating tunnels. Plants are able to absorb more water and air through these tunnels. The tunnels also help the roots to grow deeper into the soil. Earthworm droppings, called **casts**, make the soil fertile. Soil also contains very tiny living things which cannot be seen by the naked eye. They are called **microbes**. Some soil microbes help the plants to grow.

Do you know?

Earthworms help in the rotting of vegetable matter speedily and efficiently. They feed on kitchen waste such as fruit and vegetable peels, unused stems and leaves. Earthworm castings are rich in nutrients. They are soluble in water and are easily absorbed by the roots of plants. This provides good natural fertilizer for the plants.

Now you know

Fill in the blanks.

- The three main types of soil are _____ soil, _____ soil, and _____ soil.
- Soils have different colours because of _____ present in them.
- Earthworm casts make the soil _____.
- Very tiny living things which cannot be seen by naked eye are called _____.

Points to Remember

- Rocks break up into soil.
- Gravel, sand, silt and clay are different types of soil particles.
- There are three different types of soil: sandy, clayey and loamy.
- Loam is the best for growing plants.
- Soil contains minerals, humus, air and water.
- Colour of the soil depends on the minerals present in it.
- Many animals and microbes live in the soil.

100

New Words

Weathering: wearing away due to weather conditions
Loam: fertile soil of clay and sand containing humus
Crops: produce of cultivated plants

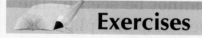

Exercises

A. Fill in the blanks with the correct option.

1. Rocks break up into smaller parts till they turn into _____.
   soil/water

2. Potters use _____ soil to make pots. loamy/clayey

3. _____ soil cannot hold water. Clayey/Sandy

4. _____ is made up of dead plants and animals. Humus/Gravel

5. _____ provide minerals needed by the plant. Rocks/Worms

6. _____ soil is suitable for most plants to grow on it .
   Sandy/Loamy

B. Name or give an example of:

1. The type of soil which cannot hold water. _____

2. One content of soil. _____

3. A natural fertilizer. _____

4. An animal which lives in the soil. _____

C. Answer these questions.

1. Name the factors which wear away rocks.

2. What is weathering of rocks?

3. How is soil formed?

4. What are the different types of soil?

5. Why is loam the best soil for growing plants?

6. How do earthworms help plants?

Task

Label the different contents of soil shown in the diagram.

Brainstorm

Visit a farm and interview the farmer. Keep a questionnaire ready to ask him. Ask him if he adds materials like plastics and glass in the natural fertilizers.

Project Idea

To show that soil is different in different places, collect some soil from your garden, the playground and the school garden. You will see the difference. The colours, the texture (feel), the size of particles, etc. will be different.

Observe the different samples and note down what you see in the table given below.

Place of collection	Colour	Texture (coarse or fine)	Size of particles (big or small)	Dry or wet

Unit 6: Natural Resources

[13] A Clean World

Our world consists of living and non-living things. The living things comprise **plants** and **animals**. The non-living things are **air, water, soil, heat** and **light**. These are also called **natural resources** as they are available in nature and can be used by people in many ways. In nature, there is a balance between these living and non-living things. This balance gets upset if one of them is disturbed.

The world consists of living and non-living things

Human beings are the most developed living things in nature, but their actions have upset the balance in nature. Their increasing number has led to a great increase in their needs. It has also led to the production of more waste all around. These wastes have spoiled the air, water and land all around us.

The addition of these harmful substances to our natural resources is called **pollution.** The substances which cause pollution are called **pollutants.**

Let us learn how we have polluted our natural resources.

Air Pollution

Air pollutants mostly consist of gases, smoke, fumes and dust. They can be small solid particles, drops of liquids or gases. The pollutants can be man-made or natural.

Causes

Smoke released from fire and burning of fuels is a major cause of air pollution. Burning of wood, coal, petrol and diesel releases smoke and fumes in the air.

Smoke from automobiles, factories, power plants and waste incinerators causes air pollution. Incinerators are used for burning waste.

Volcanoes too produce smoke, ashes and chemicals polluting air.

Pollutants produced by nuclear explosions and war explosives also affect air.

Acid rain: When fuels are burnt in factories, gases containing nitrogen, carbon and sulphur are released. These gases combine with moisture and form acids. When it rains, these acids combine with raindrops and fall on the earth. This is called **acid rain.** These acids also combine with hail, sleet and snow. Acid rain pollutes water. It kills fish. It damages crops and buildings. It destroys whatever it falls on.

Smoke from automobiles and factories cause air pollution

Smoke, ashes and chemicals from volcanoes pollute the air

Acid rain

Effects

Air pollution can cause coughs, breathing problems and burning eyes. When smoke gets mixed with fog, it produces **smog.** Smog stays close to the surface level and creates a haze, reducing visibility.

Smog

Water Pollution

Causes

People throw garbage, flowers, plastic waste, etc. in the rivers and lakes. They wash clothes, vehicles and animals.

Sewage water, water mixed with chemicals and hot water from factories are also released in the water bodies.

Chemical fertilizers and insecticides used in crop fields get mixed with rain water and flow into rivers and lakes.

All these factors cause water pollution.

105

Garbage pollutes water

Chemical wastes from factories cause water pollution

Effects

Polluted water carries harmful germs. Drinking such water causes diseases such as typhoid, diarrhoea, dysentery or cholera.

Water polluted by chemicals from factories affects aquatic life and kills aquatic animals and plants.

Soil Pollution

Causes

Soil pollution is caused by waste from various sources. Domestic waste is a very big problem. Solid waste from the industries pollutes the soil. Chemicals used as fertilizers and insecticides too cause soil pollution.

Soil pollution

Effects

Soil pollution causes loss of nutrients and reduces the fertility of the soil. It also causes soil erosion. Harmful chemicals which pollute the soil, are absorbed by plants. When these plants are eaten by us, it can cause a number of diseases.

Now you know

Fill in the blanks.

• Addition of harmful substances in our natural resources is called _____

• _____ and _____ get mixed to form smog.

• Drinking polluted water can cause _____.

Disposal of Waste

Every day, we dump a lot of solid and liquid waste in the soil. Some of these wastes are produced from living things. These include domestic wastes like fruit and vegetable peels, paper, clothes made from cotton or wool, broken wooden furniture, etc. These wastes rot and mix with the soil after some time. These wastes are called **biodegradable wastes**.

Wastes from living things are biodegradable

Wastes produced from man-made things are non-biodegradable

But wastes produced from non-living things, such as plastics, glass, metals, chemicals and synthetic fibre do not rot. They remain in the soil for a very long time and cause soil pollution. Such wastes are called **non-biodegradable wastes**.

Biodegradable and non-biodegradable wastes need different treatment. So they are first sorted out by the garbage collecting agencies.

Biodegradable wastes are dumped in large pits called **landfills**. Here they are covered with a layer of soil and allowed to rot.

Landfill

Non-biodegradable wastes like plastic and glass which can be re-used are sent to **recycling units**. Here these are melted and used to make new products. Non-biodegradable wastes which cannot be reused are sent to burning units called **incinerators**.

How we can help prevent pollution

Village panchayats, municipalities and municipal corporations are the main civic agencies which are responsible for disposing off the garbage produced by us daily.

On our part, we must try to keep our villages, towns and cities clean. We must try to reduce pollution.

Segregate wastes: Collect biodegradable and non-biodegradable wastes in separate waste bins. These can then be easily collected by the garbage collectors and sent for appropriate treatment.

You can also make a small pit in your backyard and dispose the biodegradable waste there. This waste will decompose or rot and turn into manure.

Separate waste bins for biodegradable and non-biodegradable waste

Use environment-friendly products: Use biodegradable products like cloth bags. Avoid use of plastic bags which are non-biodegradable.

Do not litter: When you go out, do not throw scrap food, empty water bottles or food wraps on the road. Take the waste home and throw it in the bins if there are no garbage bins on the way.

Save paper: Do not waste paper. A lot of trees have to be cut down to make paper.

Save trees: Plant as many trees as you can. Plants give you shade, food, etc. They also take in carbon dioxide and release oxygen.

Save fuel: Walk when you are travelling short distances. Try and use bicycles or use public transport in which many people can travel together. This will help in reducing pollution. Regular pollution check should be carried out for all vehicles.

Save energy: Switch off electrical appliances like lights, fan, TV, music system and computer when not in use. By doing this, you can save electricity.

Reduce, reuse and recycle: Remember the three R's —Reduce, Reuse and Recycle.

Reduce your needs. Do not buy things you do not need. Do not accumulate more things than you need. The more things you have, the more wastes you produce.

Buy things which can be used again and again over a long period of time. Avoid disposable things which have to be thrown away after every use.

Recycling is converting waste into reusable material. A number of wastes like old newspaper, empty glass bottles, plastics and tins can be recycled and turned into new products.

Talk to your friends and relatives about the importance of the three R's.

Fill in the blanks.

- Wastes which rot are called _____ wastes.
- Wastes which do not rot are called _____ wastes.
- The three R's of preventing pollution are _____, _____ and _____.

Do you know?

You must have seen rag-pickers scavenging garbage bins and dumping grounds. They collect recyclable wastes and sell them to recycling units to earn their livelihood. But while doing so, they expose themselves to great health risks.

Garbage usually contains both wet and dry wastes. **Wet waste** includes waste in which germs can grow. They include food wastes, dead plant and animal remains, human and animal excreta, etc. **Dry waste** includes items such as bottles, cans, clothing, plastic, wood, glass, metals and paper. It includes both recyclable and non-recyclable materials.

If dry and wet wastes are segregated, the rag-pickers would just have to pick the dry waste and avoid exposure to microbes and pollution.

109

Points to Remember

- Air pollutants consist of gases, smoke, fumes and dust.
- Smoke from fire and burning of fuels is a major cause of air pollution.
- Acid rain damages the things it falls on.
- Water pollution is caused by garbage, sewage water and chemicals.
- Polluted water causes diseases and affects aquatic life.
- Soil pollution is caused by domestic and industrial waste.
- We must try to reduce pollution.
- We must remember to reduce, reuse and recycle.

New Words

Natural resources: materials that are found in nature and are used by people in many ways

Pollution: addition of harmful substances into the environment

Pollutants: harmful substances causing pollution

Fume: gas or smoke that is not pleasant or healthy

Acid: a chemical that can damage things that come in contact with it

Smog: a mixture of smoke and fog

Dispose: to throw away

Biodegradable: a substance which can rot

Non-biodegradable: a substance which cannot rot

Landfill: a place where the garbage of a city or town is dumped

Incinerator: a furnace for burning waste

Segregate: to separate or place apart

Litter: to make messy by throwing around waste paper or other objects

110

Exercises

A. Fill in the blanks with the correct option.

1. Gases, smoke, fumes and dust are _____ pollutants.
   air/water

2. Water polluted by chemicals from factories affects _____
   life. marine/aerial

3. Waste which rots is known as _____ waste.
   biodegradable/non-biodegradable

4. Save _____ by switching off electrical gadgets.
   paper/energy

5. We should use _____ bags as they are biodegradable.
   cloth/plastic

B. Name the following.

1. Harmful substances which cause pollution _____

2. Unwanted things _____

3. Waste which cannot be decomposed _____

4. The three R's   _____

5. To convert waste into reusable material   _____

C. Answer these questions in detail.

1. Two causes of air pollution

     _____

2. Two causes of water pollution

     _____

3. Two diseases caused by polluted water

     _____

4. Two ways to prevent pollution

     _____

D. Answer these questions.

1. What is acid rain?
2. What is biodegradable waste?
3. How can you save fuel?
4. Why should you send newspapers for recycling?
5. What harm do glass bottles and metal cans cause?

Task

Colour the biodegradable waste bin and non-biodegradable waste bin with the suitable colour. Insist that everyone follows the rules of throwing the waste in the separate bins.

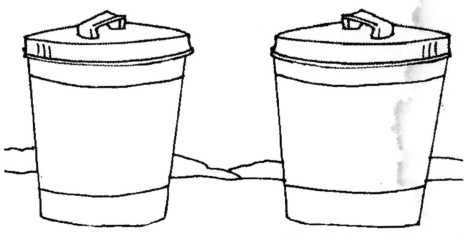

Biodegradable waste   Non-biodegradable waste

Can you think of the causes of what you can see in this picture?

Note down the causes and the solutions to the problem. Talk about it to other children during the assembly.

Project Idea

Visit a recycling centre. Take photographs if it is possible. Note down the method of recycling. Make a project using the photographs and a write-up on recycling. Try and buy things which are made from recycled materials.

112

Unit 7: Our Universe

[14] Our Earth and its Neighbours

Warm Up

Unscramble the words given in the boxes to find the correct answer.

- The oval path of the earth around the sun is known as _____. BIRTO
- The earth spins on its _____. ISAX
- The movement of the earth around the sun is known as _____. TIONVOLURE
- The instrument used to study stars and plants is known as _____. LESTECOPE

We see millions of stars twinkling in the night sky. They look like tiny spots of light. But in reality, stars are huge balls of fire. They give off heat and light.

The sun

The sun is also a star. Some stars are smaller than the sun and some are bigger than the sun. The sun is the nearest star to the earth. So, it looks bigger and brighter compared to the other stars. The glare of its light does not allow us to see the other stars during daytime.

The Sun and the Solar System

The sun has a family of eight large heavenly bodies moving around it. They are called **planets**. The eight planets are Mercury, Venus, Earth, Mars, Jupiter, Saturn, Uranus and Neptune. Together, the sun and the eight planets form the **solar system**. Each planet moves around the sun in a definite oval-shaped path called **orbit**. The planets stay in their orbits due to the attracting power of the sun. This attracting power is known as **gravity.**

The planets

In the order of their increasing distance from the sun, the planets are:

Mercury : It is the smallest planet in the solar system. The side facing the sun is very hot and the side away from the sun is extremely cold. It has craters on its surface.

Venus: It is the brightest and the hottest planet in the solar system. The atmosphere on Venus is a mixture of poisonous gases. It is also called the **morning star** or **evening star** as it shows up brightly in the morning and evening.

Earth: The earth is our home planet. It is the only known planet with water and which supports life.

The solar system

Mars: It is known as the **red planet**. Strong windstorms in Mars throw up sand and fill the air with dust. This dust gives it the red colour.

Jupiter: It is the biggest of all the planets. It has thick clouds of gas which form bands around it. A huge **red spot** can be seen in the clouds of Jupiter.

Saturn: It is surrounded by prominent rings formed by ice, rocks and dust.

Uranus: Uranus is the third largest planet in the solar system, and is known as a gas giant.

Neptune: Neptune experiences strong winds and storms. The winds on Neptune are the fastest in the solar system.

Satellites

There are some heavenly bodies which travel around the planets. They are called **satellites** or moons. Some planets have more than one moon. The earth has only one satellite. It is named as the **moon.**

The moon does not have an atmosphere. Its surface is also full of craters and mountains.

The moon

An artificial satellite orbiting the earth

Artificial satellites

Artificial satellites are scientific instruments sent by scientists to orbit around the earth. The artificial satellites are of great use and serve many purposes.

Man-made satellites take photographs and send information to the earth about storms, clouds, weather, etc. They also help in transferring telephone calls and sending radio and television signals. Artificial satellites also assist in the navigation of ships and aeroplanes. They are also used to monitor crops, locate mineral deposits, identify sources of pollution and study its effects.

115

Now you know

Fill in the blanks.

- The sun is a _____ .
- The sun and the eight planets which revolve around the sun form the _____ system.
- _____ is the biggest planet.
- Artificial _____ are sent by scientists to orbit around the earth.

Inside the Earth

Millions of years ago, our earth was a ball of gas and dust. It was a hot glowing ball. Gradually, the outside of the earth began to cool. As the outside part cooled, it became hard. The inside part is still very hot even today.

The hard outer layer of the earth is called the **crust**. The continents and the oceans are on the crust.

Under the crust is a rocky layer called the **mantle**. The rocks in the mantle contain different types of minerals. The mantle becomes hotter as it goes deeper.

Beneath the mantle is a layer of hot, molten metal called the **core**. The outer core contains liquid iron and nickel. The inner core contains solid iron and nickel.

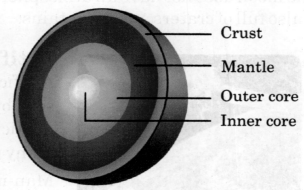

Inside the earth

Volcano

The mantle is mostly solid rock, but flows like melted plastic. Because of the extreme temperature and pressure in the core, the rocks of the lower mantle melt. This liquid rock is called **magma**. The magma moves to the earth's surface through weak spots in the crust.

Upon reaching the surface, it releases heat, gases and rock, with great force. This is called a **volcanic eruption.**

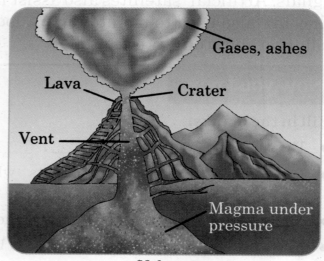

Volcano

116

The magma that comes out of the ground is called **lava**. It hardens after cooling and piles up in the shape of a cone with a tunnel in the middle. Volcanoes may also release poisonous gases and a cloud of ash.

Volcanoes can also erupt inside water. There are many volcanoes in the world. Most of them do not erupt anymore. They are called **extinct volcanoes**. Some are sleeping volcanoes and may erupt again. They are called **dormant volcanoes**. Only a few volcanoes are **active** and keep erupting.

Now you know

Fill in the blanks.

- The continents and the oceans lie on the _____ of the earth.
- The molten rock in the lower mantle is known as _____ .
- Only a few volcanoes are _____ and keep erupting.

Movements of the Earth

Rotation

You know that the earth spins around its own axis. The imaginary axis is slightly tilted. One end of the axis is the **North Pole** and the other end is the **South Pole**. The spinning of the earth around its axis is known as **rotation.**

Day and night: Rotation of the earth causes day and night. In the morning, when the sky is bright, our side of the earth faces the sun. In the evening, when the sky is dark, our side of the earth turns away from the sun. The earth takes twenty-four hours to complete one rotation.

Revolution

You also know that the earth also travels around the sun in a fixed oval-shaped path called the **orbit**. This movement of the earth is known as **revolution.** The time taken by earth to complete one revolution is $365\frac{1}{4}$ days.

The earth is divided into two equal parts called **hemispheres** by an imaginary line in the middle of the earth. This line is called the **equator**. The northern half is called the **northern hemisphere** and the southern half is called the **southern hemisphere**.

Night   Day

Seasons: The earth's revolution and its tilted axis cause **seasons**.

When the North Pole is tilted towards the sun, the northern hemisphere receives most of the sunlight and hence has summer. At the same time, the southern hemisphere which is away from the sun does not get much sunlight and hence has winter. When the South Pole is tilted towards the sun, the southern hemisphere receives more sunlight and has summer. The northern hemisphere which is away from the sun has winter.

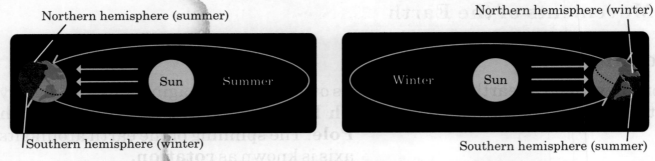

Summer and winter in the northern and southern hemisphere

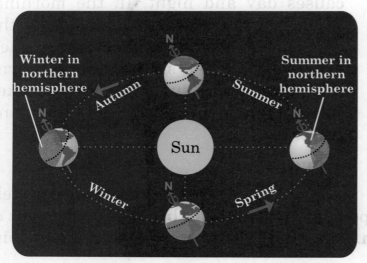

Change of seasons in the northern hemisphere

Between these two seasons in a hemisphere, there comes a period when it is neither too hot nor too cold. The autumn season comes at the end of summer. Similarly, at the end of winter comes the spring season. During these seasons the weather is neither too hot nor too cold.

The equator, which is in the middle of the earth always receives the same amount of sunlight throughout the year and is always hot.

Points to Remember

- Stars are huge balls of fire. They give off heat and light.

- Heavenly bodies that travel around the sun are called planets.

- Heavenly bodies which travel around the planets are called satellites.

- The outermost layer of the earth is called the crust and the innermost part is the core. The middle layer is the mantle.

- When a volcano explodes, it throws out pieces of rocks and pushes out lava.

- Volcanoes are of three types: active, dormant and extinct.

- The earth's rotation causes day and night.

- The earth's revolution and its tilted axis causes seasons.

 ## New Words

Planet: a large heavenly object that moves around the sun or another star

Solar system: the sun and the planets moving around it

Gravity: the force by which an object attracts other bodies around it

Orbit: the curved path in which a planet or a satellite moves around the sun or planet

Satellites: heavenly bodies which travel around the planets

Magma: hot liquid matter under the earth's surface

Lava: hot, melted rock that erupts from a volcano

Eruption: bursting out

Pole: either end of a planet's, star's or satellite's axis

Hemisphere: either of two halves of the earth

Equator: the imaginary circle around the middle of the earth

Exercises

A. Fill in the blanks with correct option.

1. The layer of hot molten metal inside the earth is called _____.
   mantle/core

2. Sleeping volcanoes are called _____ volcanoes.
   extinct/dormant

3. The time taken for one revolution by the earth is _____days.
   $356\frac{1}{4}$ /$365\frac{1}{4}$

4. When the North Pole is tilted towards the sun, the southern hemisphere has _____. summer/winter

5. The _____ receives the same amount of sunlight throughout the year. North Pole/ equator

B. Name the following.

1. Heavenly bodies which travel around planets _____

2. The molten rock deep down inside the earth _____

3. Two ends through which the axis of the earth passes _____

4. Imaginary line which divides the earth into two equal parts _____

5. Volcanoes which do not erupt anymore _____

C. Draw neat labelled diagrams of the following.

1. The different layers of the earth
2. A volcano
3. Earth showing the two hemispheres
4. Summer in northern hemisphere

D. Answer these questions.

1. What are artificial satellites?
2. How do day and night occur?
3. What causes seasons?

120

Task

Match the following.

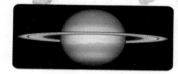

Saturn

Satellite

Volcano

Telescope

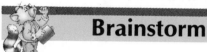

Brainstorm

What is the season during Christmas in the northern hemisphere and in the southern hemisphere?

Project Idea

Find out the names of five artificial satellites, the year they were launched and their main functions. Present it in a tabular form. Collect their pictures from the internet and paste them around the table.

Test Paper I

A. Fill in the blanks with the correct option.

1. Meat and fish are rich in _____. proteins/carbohydrates
2. Teeth used for chewing and grinding are _____. incisors/molars
3. If the gas from a cooking gas cylinder leaks, you must _____ the windows. open/close
4. Do not _____ near the door of the train. stand/walk
5. Fibres are _____ into threads. yarn/spun
6. _____ walls keep the house cool. Thick/Thin
7. In _____, the molecules are closely packed. liquids/solids
8. The flat broad surface of the leaf is called the _____. leaf blade/petiole
9. _____ have flippers to swim in the water. Dolphins/Ducks
10. Trees which grow in marshy lands are known as _____. mangroves/epiphytes

B. Tick (✓) mark the correct sentence and cross (✗) out the wrong one.

1. Canning is a method of food preservation.
2. Bile helps to digest carbohydrates.
3. You must not use sharp objects to hurt others.
4. Jute is obtained from coconut fibres.
5. Slate is used as a flooring material.
6. Substances which dissolve in a liquid are soluble in it.
7. The food prepared by the plants is in the form of proteins.
8. Bats are not birds.
9. Spines in a cactus plant prevent the loss of water.
10. Starches and sugar are energy giving foods.

C. Answer in one sentence.

1. Name the nutrients required by our body.
2. What is meant by digestion of food?
3. Why should you not listen to music while riding a bicycle?
4. What is cutting of fleece called?
5. What is building material?
6. What is solubility?
7. What does a plant require to make food?
8. What is habitat?
9. Name a plant which is completely submerged in water.
10. How many teeth do children have?

D. Match the following.

1. iron
2. mouth
3. bicycle
4. cocoon
5. engineer
6. water
7. photosynthesis
8. amphibian
9. neem tree
10. first aid

a. saliva
b. universal solvent
c. silkworm
d. helmet
e. constructs a house
f. mineral
g. can live on land and in water
h. process of making food in plants
I. first medical help
j. deciduous tree

E. Draw and label.

1. Structure of a tooth
2. Parts of a leaf

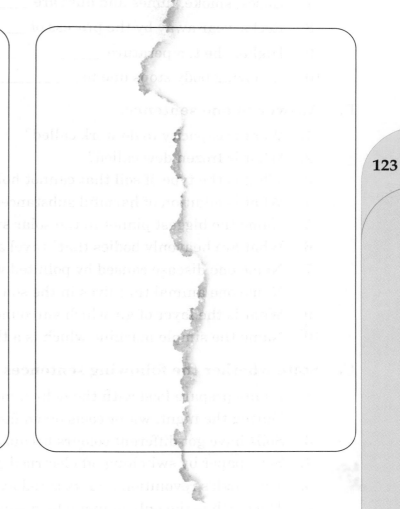

Test Paper II

A. Fill in the blanks with the correct option.

1. When a ball is thrown up, it falls down because of _____ force. muscular/gravitational

2. The _____ breeze blows from the sea towards the land during the day. land/sea

3. Earthworm casts make the soil _____. fertile/polluted

4. Wastes which rot are called _____ wastes. biodegradable/non-biodegradable

5. The molten rock in the lower mantle is known as _____. magma/lava

6. Imaginary line which divides the earth into two equal parts is called _____. rotation/equator

7. Gases, smoke, fumes and dust are _____ pollutants. air/water

8. Rocks wear away by the process of _____. weathering/watering

9. Higher the temperature, _____ is the rate of evaporation. faster/slower

10. A moving body stops due to _____ force. gravitational/frictional

B. Answer in one sentence.

1. What is capacity to do work called?
2. What is frozen dew called?
3. What is the type of soil that cannot hold water called?
4. What is addition of harmful substances in our natural resources called?
5. Name the biggest planet in the solar system.
6. What are heavenly bodies that travel around the planets called?
7. Name one disease caused by polluted water.
8. Name one animal that lives in the soil.
9. What is the layer of air which surrounds the earth called?
10. Name the simple machine which is a thin cone with a spiral ridge around it.

C. State whether the following sentences are true or false.

1. Plants prepare food with the help of mechanical energy. _____
2. During the night, water cools down faster than land. _____
3. Soils have got different colours because of the nutrients present in them. _____
4. Save paper by switching off electrical gadgets. _____
5. The earth's revolution and its tilted axis causes seasons. _____
6. The earth is the only planet which supports life. _____
7. Acid rain destroys whatever it falls on. _____

8. Soil contains air. _____

9. Light is a form of energy. _____

10. The process in which water changes from liquid form to gas is called condensation. _____

D. Match the following.

1.	simple machine	a.	unwanted things
2.	sun	b.	telecommunication
3.	humus	c.	surrounded by rings
4.	smog	d.	made up of dead plants and animals
5.	artificial satellite	e.	makes work easy
6.	Saturn	f.	smoke mixed with fog
7.	waste	g.	causes changes in weather
8.	clayey soil	h.	frozen dewdrops
9.	frost	i	frozen water
10.	ice	j.	used to make pots

E. Draw and label.

1. One simple machine
2. Summer in Northern Hemisphere